Routledge Revivals

The Music of Spain

First published in 1920, *The Music of Spain* deals with historical periods, schools and style and appears to embrace everything related to music provided it affects or is affected by Spain in some degree, no matter how small or insignificant. The period extends from the sixteenth century to the early twentieth century and the author encircles his subject in a huge ring or parenthesis that opens with Antonio Cabezon, the Spanish Bach (according to Pedrell) and closes with the gypsy dancer and singer Pastora Imperio, queen of the Spanish "varieties" stage of today. It brings themes like Spain and music; the land of joy; and from George Borrow to Mary Garden. This book is an important historical reference for students and scholars of history of music, Spanish music.

The Music of Spain

Carl Van Vechten

First published in 1920
by Kegan Paul, Trench, Trubner & Co., Ltd.

This edition first published in 2024 by Routledge
4 Park Square, Milton Park, Abingdon, Oxon, OX14 4RN

and by Routledge
605 Third Avenue, New York, NY 10017

Routledge is an imprint of the Taylor & Francis Group, an informa business

© Carl Van Vechten, 1920

All rights reserved. No part of this book may be reprinted or reproduced or utilised in any form or by any electronic, mechanical, or other means, now known or hereafter invented, including photocopying and recording, or in any information storage or retrieval system, without permission in writing from the publishers.

Publisher's Note
The publisher has gone to great lengths to ensure the quality of this reprint but points out that some imperfections in the original copies may be apparent.

Disclaimer
The publisher has made every effort to trace copyright holders and welcomes correspondence from those they have been unable to contact.

A Library of Congress record exists under LCCN: 34009726

ISBN: 978-1-032-76062-9 (hbk)
ISBN: 978-1-003-47691-7 (ebk)
ISBN: 978-1-032-76064-3 (pbk)

Book DOI 10.4324/9781003476917

MARY GARDEN AS CARMEN, ACT IV
from a photograph by Mishkin

THE
MUSIC OF SPAIN

BY
CARL VAN VECHTEN

WITH PREFACE AND NOTES
BY
PEDRO G. MORALES

LONDON :
KEGAN PAUL, TRENCH, TRUBNER & CO., LTD.
BROADWAY HOUSE, 68-74 CARTER LANE, E.C.
1920

" Il faut méditerraniser la musique."
                                            Nietzsche.

For Blanche Knopf

CONTENTS

	PAGE
PREFACE	ix
NOTES	xxi
SPAIN AND MUSIC	7
THE LAND OF JOY	113
FROM GEORGE BORROW TO MARY GARDEN	125
INDEX	161

ILLUSTRATIONS

MARY GARDEN AS CARMEN, ACT IV	*Front.*
	FACING PAGE
TARQUINIA TARQUINI AS CONCHITA	20
LA ARGENTINA	36
THOMAS BRETON	96
DOLORETES	120
ZULOAGA'S PORTRAIT OF LUCIENNE BRÉVAL AS CARMEN, ACT II	148
OLIVE FREMSTAD AS CARMEN, ACT I	154
AMADEO VIVES	104

PREFACE

By PEDRO G. MORALES.

THE idea of the author of this book is perhaps better expressed in the title of its first chapter, " Spain and Music," than by *The Music of Spain*, for the author does not deal solely with the subject in relation to historical periods, schools, or style, as is often the case with books of this kind. The present work appears to embrace everything related to music, provided it affects or is affected by Spain in some degree, no matter how small or insignificant. The period extends from the XVI. Century to the present day, or, in order to make the reader realize at once the true character of his work, I should say that the author encircles his subject in a huge ring or parenthesis that opens with Antonio Cabezon, the Spanish Bach (according to Pedrell) and closes with the gypsy dancer and singer, Pastora Imperio, queen of the Spanish " varieties " stage of to-day. The task might seem at first sight injudiciously ambitious, and from the point of view of bibliographical routine, incorrect and perhaps insurmountable, but Mr. C. Van

PREFACE—*continued*

Vechten has accomplished his purpose with exceptional ability and success within the scope of a comparatively small book. If it is true that he only touches " en passant " many points of far-reaching importance, it is also true that there is not a single point of interest in his wide scheme which he leaves untouched. Those particularly concerned with the study of Nationality in Music and the *musicologue* and folk-lore student in general have to welcome in Mr. Van Vechten's book a work long needed and expected in these days of sudden and ever increasing hispanophilia; a work that constitutes the most complete guide the student of all types of Spanish music could wish for at the present time. It is written in a breathless but well-sustained style, and though essentially non-critical, contains many wise and subtle critical remarks, besides endless reliable and curious information.

Erudites and scholars have had always at their disposal special works, such as *Le Mysticisme musical espagnol au XVIe. Siècle,* and others mentioned in their proper place, the above being by Mr. Henri Collet, one of the greatest living authorities on ancient and modern Spanish music; but the public in general have been, until recently, in a very different position.

It was only five years ago that, as one of the many curious effects of the universal upheaval produced by the Great War, the attention of the principal belligerent countries was converted to the long neglected subject of Spanish music. In reality, a European reaction took place on behalf of Spanish art, music specially, as it was then the least known abroad of all the manifestations of our artistic life. Whether such reaction was based on pure motives is a question that does not concern us here, but there are two circumstances in relation to that fact well worth recording. First: The general interest in the music of Spain continues, and is gradually increasing* since the cessation of the war. Second: The said reaction coincided with the breaking into life of the "renacimiento" that Pedrell and Albéniz had initiated years ago, each of them in their respective spheres of action, for Pedrell is essentially a pedagogue, while Albéniz was just the opposite. He had a higher mission; he was an inspirer.

More newspaper articles on the subject of Spanish music and folk-lore have appeared during the last five years in all Europe, than during the previous fifty or sixty years together. Yet the general public is still very far from being properly enlightened on this subject, as the value of the said writings (this being said without

*The modern French composers, especially Ravel and Debussy, had always been particularly interested in the music of Spain. This is confirmed by many of their compositions, and their admirable attitude towards the Spanish composers and students living in Paris before the war. As I have said elsewhere: "Spanish music was performed and acknowledged in France as an artistic achievement before it was recognised as such even in Spain."

PREFACE—*continued*

malice) is not always in keeping with their profusion. To this state of affairs, other causes have also contributed.

Inaccuracy and misunderstanding is the prominent feature of a great part of the literature on Spain produced during the last eighty years or so, especially in its reference to our folk-lore and music. Travellers and *art-explorers* seem to get always more in touch with our professional exponents of national songs and dances, than with the people, and their observations suffer in consequence. This most regrettable occurrence can be excused and explained, for it is not so easy, for instance, to come across a group of peasants singing and dancing in their native surroundings, as to pay professionals (not always good and genuine) to arrange a " juerga " or " fiesta " for the amusement of tourists. To give a full explanation of all the local terms that appear in the course of this book, to point out the small but important errors in national *nuances* to be found in the many quotations from different writers that the author so wisely introduces in his text, would be beyond the limits and the non-critical character of this Introduction. Nevertheless, I must call the readers' attention to the fact that the appreciations of artists appearing in this book, such as those by Chabrier, Arthur Symons, and especially Raul Laparra, are more trustworthy and useful than those by travellers and literateurs, in the strict sense of these words. Æsthetic sensibility is a far better medium of judgment in these matters than scientific analysis. In this respect, special mention must be made of Havelock Ellis' subtle observation (pp. 65-119): "The finest Spanish dancing is at once killed or degraded by the presence of an indifferent or unsympathetic public, and that is probably why it cannot be transplanted, but remains local." Such would be the case with the *gauchos* of South America, as they improvise "coplas," or with the Hungarian gypsy as he extemporises his *Czardas*. But is it not after all, the same phenomena that takes place when a great artist finds himself powerless against the disastrous physical and moral effect produced by an indifferent or unsympathetic audience? Real art, both in its most elemental or highest developed form, is the result of inspiration, and inspiration in its turn, the result of undisturbed idleness of mind, unconscious concentration. But let us turn to our main subject. "Spain and Music" represents to-day the most successful attempt made outside Spain to *popularize* the cause of Spanish music, and what is still more important, to foster the understanding of the Spanish character through the most direct, faithful, though subtle and evasive, medium, of popular expression: music, dance, song, something individuals cannot invent: elemental rhythm. Such effort can but inspire the greatest sympathy and gratitude to all those, professionals or amateurs, who have the progress of Spanish art at heart, for is it not evident that the author has treated his subject not only with efficiency and honesty, but with real " amore " ?

Read the chapter, " The Land of Joy." He works himself up to such a pitch of excitement, that he exclaims : " Let us hope that Spain will have no artistic reawakening (p. 124)." Well, his own enthusiasm makes him forget or ignore that what he has been describing in such fluent and spirited words, is (as well as the whole *raison d'être* of his book) a proof of an artistic reawakening, the manifestations of which are to be found nowadays not only in the concert-room and theatre, but in the music-hall and the " café-chantant " of our country. Popular music in Spain (including dance and song) has undergone a long period of decadence, such as that which we will call here " musica seria " or " musica sinfonica." The two cases, nevertheless, differ in great measure, for the above-mentioned style degenerated through the influence of the can-can and the French " coupletiste " vogue that once swept Europe like a plague, while the latter did not exist in reality (the Sixteenth Century school excepted), until the days of Pedrell and Albéniz, thanks to the incurable " Italianism " from which their predecessors suffered from the beginning to the end of their lives.

One might have wished that the climax of enthusiasm to which we have just referred had been provoked by Falla's "Noches en los Jardines de España," or Albéniz's "Iberia." (Has the author heard Arthur Rubinstein play any of those piano pieces ? . . .) But let us trust the Spanish proverb that says : " All roads lead to Rome," and hope that the spicy " picarismo " of Quinito Valverde will convert Mr. Van Vechten to the exquisite subtlety of Falla and Albéniz, just as the warm, popular " cantares" of my country have lead many a foreigner to read and never forget the sublime sweetness of San Juan de la Cruz's poetry. Surely the miracle will take place (if it has not been already accomplished), for everything good can be expected of one who says : " What we have been thinking of all these years in accepting the imitation and ignoring the actuality, I don't know . . . . How these devilish Spaniards have been able to keep it up all this time, I can't imagine." (p. 123.)

Bravo ! This is the right spirit. This will bear good fruit. What was a dead wall, and could not lead anywhere, was the old-fashioned attitude, with all its natural consequences, of considering " Carmen " the *quintessence* of everything Spanish. Of that quite incontestable truth, Mr. Van Vechten does not seem to be quite fully convinced. He is aware of our views on this point, but does not appear to accept them without a certain amount of reluctancy, as he shows (very discreetly indeed) in the last part of the book, *From George Borrow to Mary Garden*. " Carmen," to begin with, is not a prototype, but a very extraordinary type of Spanish woman. The novel of Merimée, is true to life, but as arranged for the stage, it is only a grotesque display of absurdities, an agglomeration of inaccurate details. The atmosphere thus created is false. The music of Bizet is so original that everybody thought after its first success that it was purely Spanish, and this belief still remains. But the case is that of the immense variety of popular melodies to be found in Spain, the great composer, faithful to the intended local colour of the *libretto*, only used besides a rhythm of Havanera, two or three Andalusian tunes, which in his hands forcibly become French, as the development goes on. Any of the piano music of Albéniz, for instance, " Evocation," which is built on original ideas, is more Spanish in feeling than Bizet's version of themes recognised as popular. The French composer carried the music of Spain in his ear for a certain purpose ; Albéniz had it in his heart, by the " gift of heaven." To these words, I had occasion to write some time ago, I may add that the Spanish woman is the most unselfish and enduring being on earth. Every " gitana " or " manola," no matter how low she may have fallen, bears the seed of fidelity. ready to blossom, deeply rooted in her heart. The operatic character, Spanish *par excellence*, is not " Carmen," but "Salud," the heroine of Manuel de Falla's opera, "La Vida Breve."

Why " Spanish religious music is perhaps not distinctively Spanish." (p. 39.) Everything that betrays the characteristics of the various elements constituting the Spanish race, is Spanish, be it Moorish, Gothic, Celtic, etc. Our religious music of the XVI. Century is as essentially Spanish as the art of Zurbaran and that of Herrera in San Lorenzo del Escorial, and as the playing of Pablo Casals, free from any trace of Orientalism, is essentially Spanish for its sobriety and sound perfection. Spanish are the sunny orchards of Andalusia, and the arid land of Castilla, the grey and dreamy mountains of Asturias, and so can be the various moods of the Spanish soul, grey, dreamy, arid, sunny . . . .

The exulting way in which Jacinto Benavente (the author of "Los Intereses Creados," and many other masterful dramatic works) praises the gypsy, Pastora Imperio, might seem outrageous to English readers, but it is not so. Benavente knows the exact meaning of words; Pastora Imperio is the very essence of rhythm. To see her appear on the stage is a revelation. She has discovered or received from God as a gift, a new art : the art of walking. She is an artist-dancer, whose movements and poses are in themselves pictures and musical compositions. Yet, I fear, she would not be understood in this country. There is something inherent in the Eng-

xviii   PREFACE—*continued*

lish people that prevents them from grasping the sense of the real Southern Spanish dancing, independent of local colour and surroundings; perhaps because there is nothing acrobatic in it. Its ideal is inner emotion, rhythmical stability, ecstasy.

The pronouncement that Spanish* is not an easy tongue to sing (p. 111), must not remain unchallenged. There are comparatively very few Spanish operas, simply because we had not in the old days composers capable of writing them. All languages are good for singing, excepting in the case of translations. The failure of Goyescas is due, not to the Spanish language, but to the fact that modern music conceived and written for the piano, cannot be made vocal by (allow me the expression), injecting words into it. The idea of making an opera with those piano pieces was a sin of commercialism, which met with the fate it well deserves.

In reading Mr. Van Vechten's work, as well as this Introduction, some might think we have given undue importance to the subject of popular music. The case is this: The modern Russian school has been discovered after it was a *fait accompli;* that of Spain has been discovered just recently, still in a very tender

---

*Spanish is the nearest language to Italian. It does not contain nasal sounds like French and Portuguese, neither the compound vowels, as in French, English and German.

PREFACE—*continued*

period of formation, a most interesting situation arising from this, both happy and unhappy circumstance. The public and critics find themselves able to watch almost from the very beginning the gradual growth of a new school of art. The poor composer, on the other hand, finds himself overburdened with responsibility. He feels the paralysing effect of the expectation he has to face, and has to work under the pressure of the demand he is called upon to satisfy prematurely and suddenly.* Another difficulty is that he has to address his public (I refer to foreign countries) in an idiom they hardly know, or what is worse, an idiom of which they have acquired wrong notions and confused ideas. Is the importance of Albeniz, not only as the founder of our modern school, but in relation to the piano literature of all times, fully recognized ? It just begins to be so, but he has not come altogether into his own. His music is still seldom played, not because of its exceptional technical difficulties, but because the interpreters find themselves embarrassed with its idiom. There are musical *nuances* and peculiarities of rhythm that have to be felt through self-identification with their origin, for they cannot be explained with words or marks of expression, a problem attached to all new types of music until their interpretation can be based on tradition. The modern school of Spain, as that of Russia, is definitely founded on National

Music. The public, in order to understand the progressive development of our composers' ideals, must understand first the musical idiom of our people, and to achieve that they must be acquainted and in sympathy with all the spontaneous manifestations of their temperament. Therefore, in order to foster the cause of modern Spanish music, all the elements of information, musical and otherwise, that may contribute to its comprehension, must be presented to the public, for the time being, dished up together (just as an *olla podrida* or *paella*), in other words, as in the present book and in this Introduction, in an apparent but really well-intentioned and carefully thought-out disorder.

PEDRO G. MORALES.

NOTES
By PEDRO G. MORALES

Vide Page 34.) That style of song peculiar to Andalusia, called "flamenco" (Flemish), for unknown reasons, is essentially Moorish. It is called also "gitano," but only because the gypsy excells in it. When designed as "cante jondo" (slang for hondo—deep), reference is made to its emotional character and the depth of feeling displayed in its rendering. This is frequently carried to a comic degree of exaggeration.

(Page 38.) The affinity between negro and Spanish music is too far fetched. The negro element to be found at times in certain dances and songs must be regarded as a degeneration, a colonial disease from the bye-gone days of the Cuban *manigua*.

Page 56.) The "sevillanas" are not "danced on certain days before the high altar of the cathedral at Seville." The dance of the *Seises* (Lord Roseberry possesses a picture of it by Gonzalo Bilbao) is more as A. Symons describes it : " A kind of solemn minuet." (*Vide* Turina's piano pieces "Rincones de Sevilla.") *Sevillanas* are the *seguidillas*, as danced in Sevilla. In La Mancha they are called *manchegas*, etc., etc.

Valera was right in resenting the title, "The Land of the Castanets." (Page 34.) He did so just because he was cultured. We all join hands with him. We reject that title, among other reasons, because it is insufficient to describe Spain.

(Page 61.) *Fandango* is the name of an old dance, and it is only metaphorically that the word is employed to denote a raw or a noisy gathering of people dancing and singing. The word Bachanale does not convey the same idea as "fandango" in a figurative sense. *Bacarme* would be better, but not exact.

(Page 69.) The popular song in Galicia is not the *seguidilla*, but tue *muñeira* or gallegada, a 6-8, that has a great melodic similarity to one of Gluck's Airs de Ballet, in "Iphigenia in Aulis."

NOTES—*continued*

(Page 80.) Juan del Enzina, poet and musician. His piece "Placida y Victoriano," was played in Rome in 1512. He was in the service of the second Duke of Alva, and later on became a canon of León, where he died. He is mainly known as a dramatist.

(Page 16.) To the list of compositions suggested by Spain to composers of other nationalities, with which the author (for his own amusement) enriches his vast store of information, I should add: Next to Delibes's "Les Filles de Cadix," "The Little Belles of Seville," by Cyril Scott. In the domain of Chamber Music, of all works, Elgar's piano quintet and E. Goosen junior's Spanish Nocturne for Cello; immediately after, Ravel's "Rapsodie Espagnole," Lord Berners' Fantaisie Espagnole; and among the operas, Frederic d'Erlanger's "Inez Mendo." The list of Spanish operas may be increased with the following : "El Final de Don Alvaro," by Conrado del Campo ; "Avapies," by the same and Barrios ; "Balada de Carnaval," by Vives, and Pedrell's "El Comte Arnau." In other respects, certain omissions must be pointed out, for instance : "Eros," an orchestral poeme, by Oscar Esplà ; a piano quintet and a piano sextet, by Turin, of which I have given the first performances in England ; the names of Arregi Guridi, La Vina, composers; those of the Spanish, Kreisler, Manuel, Quiroga, Juan Manen, great violinist and composer; Graciela Pareto, the celebrated soprano ; the 'cellist, Gaspar Cassado ; the musicologues, Rafael Mitjana, Jesus Aroca, F. Gascué ; and among the critic-musicologue-composers, Manuel Manrique de Lara ; and the youngest of all, but not the least distinguished, Adolfo Salazar, an active pioneer of the Spanish revival and all modern tendencies in art.

The following names besides those appearing elsewhere in the course of this book will complete a list of modern composers whose works have been performed lately at the concerts of the Sociedad Nacional de Musica, Orquesta Sinfonica and Orquesta Filarmonica in Madrid : F. Aula, F. Alis, J. Arriaga, J. Blanco Recio, F. Calés, J. Cassado, J. Frigola, Gomez, J. M. Guervos, J. R. Manzanares, P. G. Morales, J. Francés, A. Gaos, Moreno Torroba, E. Noqués, Lopez Roberts, J. Pahissa, Maria Rodrigo, P. José, A. de San Sebastian, P. Antonio Soler, T. J. Valdovinos, P. Valls, A. Vila.

---

*Nearly 200 new works, by native composers, have been performed in Madrid during the last four years, mostly at the Socieded Nacional de Musica. How many of these works could be heard with approbation abroad, I am not in a position to say. This society was created five years ago at the death of another one, which had been for some time in existence, called Sociedad Wagneriana. The new one has proved far more useful to our artistic interests and ideals ; it is the very soul of the actual revival, and in connection with it, it would be unjust not to mention the distinguished amateur, Don Miguel Salvador, its first president and one of its founders.

NOTE BY THE EDITOR

The author of the Preface of this book, after receiving a University Education in Spain, studied music at the Royal College, London, and has since identified himself with the musical profession in England, English music being as familiar to him as that of his own country. He was responsible for the first Orchestral and Chamber Music Concerts of Spanish Music in England, which took place in London on March 22nd, 1918, and in Cambridge, March 4th, 1919.

He is perhaps better known in Spain as a Poet than as a Musician, and is a contributor of articles on artistic and literary subjects to both Spanish and English periodicals.

His published compositions include Violin Pieces and Songs. Among the best known of these are "Esquisse Andalouse" for Violin and Orchestra (played for the first time in London by Kreisler), and the Song "Mañana de Prima vera," in which, as in his poems "Germenes," he shows himself to possess the introspective rather than the external characteristics of the Andalusian, a peculiarity which his identification with English life has not in the least diminished or attenuated.

Spain and Music

IT has seemed to me at times that Oscar Hammerstein was gifted with almost prophetic vision. He it was who imagined the glory of Times Square, in New York. Theatre after theatre he fashioned in what was then a barren district—and presently the crowds and the hotels came. He foresaw that French opera, given in the French manner, would be successful again in New York, and he upset the calculations of all the wiseacres by making money even with *Pelléas et Mélisande*, that esoteric collaboration of Belgian and French art, which in the latter part of the season of 1907-8 attained a record of seven performances at the Manhattan Opera House, all to audiences as vast and as devoted as those which attend the sacred festivals of *Parsifal* at Bayreuth. And he had announced for presentation during the season of 1908-9 (and again the following season) a Spanish opera called *La Dolores*. The score called for a large number of guitar players. "More than I could get together readily," he told me. "I should have been obliged to have engaged all the barbers in New York." . Raoul Laparra spoke to me with enthusiasm about the orchestration of *La Dolores ;* "The guitars produce an extraordinary effect." If Hammerstein had carried out his intention he would have had another honour thrust upon him, that of having been beforehand in the production of modern Spanish opera in New York, an honour which, in the circumstances, must go to Mr. Gatti-Casazza. Strictly speaking *Goyescas* was not the first Spanish opera to be given in New York, although it was the first to be produced at the Metropolitan Opera House. *Il Guarany*, by Antonio Carlos Gomez, a Portuguese born in Brazil, was performed by the " Milan Grand Opera Company " during a three weeks' season at the Star Theatre in the fall of 1884. An air from this opera is still in the répertoire of many sopranos. To go still farther back, two of Manuel Garcia's operas, sung of course in Italian, *l'Amante Astuto* and *La Figlia dell'Aria*, were performed at the Park Theatre in 1825 with Maria Garcia—later to become the celebrated Mme. Malibran—in the principal rôles. More recently an itinerant Italian opéra-bouffe company, which gravitated from the Park Theatre—not the same edifice that harboured Garcia's company!—to various play-houses on the Bowery, included three zarzuelas in its répertoire. One of these, the popular *La Gran Via*, was announced for performance,* but my records are dumb on the

---

*I heard a performance of *La Gran Via* in Italian at the People's Theatre on the Bowery, July 1, 1918. The work is a favourite with itinerant Italian opéra-bouffe companies, probably on account of the very delightful *Pickpockets' Jota* in which the rogues outwit policemen in a dozen different ways. This strikes a truly picaresque note, redolent of folk-lore. The music of this number, too, is the best in the score aside from the *Tango de la Menegilda*. This performance was primitive and certainly not in the Spanish manner but it was very gay and delightful from beginning to end.

subject and I am not certain that it was actually given. There are probably other instances.* Hammerstein had previously produced two operas *about* Spain when he opened his first Manhattan Opera House on the site now occupied by Macy's Department Store with Moszkowski's *Boabdil*, quickly followed by Beethoven's *Fidelio*. The malagueña from *Boabdil* is still a favourite *morceau* with restaurant orchestras, and I believe I have heard the entire ballet suite performed by the Chicago Orchestra under the direction of Theodore Thomas. New York's real occupation by the Spaniards, however, occurred after the close of Mr. Hammerstein's brilliant seasons, although the earlier vogue of Carmencita, whose celebrated portrait by Sargent in the Luxembourg Gallery in Paris will long preserve her fame, the interest in the highly-coloured paintings by Sorolla and Zuloaga, many of which are still on exhibition in private and public galleries in New York, the success here achieved, in varying degrees, by such singing artists as Emilio de Gogorza, Andres de Segurola, and Lucrezia Bori,

*Since the performance of *Goyescas* there have been many instances. During the season of 1916-17 at least two attempts were made by Spanish companies to give New York a taste of the zarzuela. In December at the Amsterdam Opera House Arrieta's *Marina* and Chapí's *El Puñao de Rosas* were sung on one evening and Valverde's *El Pobre Valbuena* and somebody else's *America para los Americanos* on another. In April a company came to the Garden Theatre and gave Chapí's *La Tempestad* and perhaps some others. Both of these experiments were made in the most primitive manner and were foredoomed to failure. . . . *The Land of Joy* was the first Spanish musical piece of any pretension (save the dull *Goyescas*) to be presented in New York.

the performances of the piano works of Albéniz, Turina, and Granados by such pianists as Ernest Schelling, George Copeland, and Leo Ornstein, and the amazing Spanish dances of Anna Pavlova (who in attempting them was but following in the footsteps of her great predecessors of the nineteenth century, Fanny Elssler and Taglioni), all fanned the flames. I should also speak of Lola Montez, who danced, acted, lectured, and died in America. Her pretensions to Spanish blood were mostly pretensions. Her father was the son of Sir Edward Gilbert of Limerick, although she had some Spanish blood on her mother's side. She spent some time in Spain and studied Spanish dancing there, but there is no evidence that she ever achieved proficiency in this art. . . . I believe both Otero and La Tortajada have appeared in the United States. But neither of these women could help the cause abroad of Spanish music or dancing. Of these two I can speak personally as I have seen them both. Elvira de Hidalgo, a Spanish soprano, sang a few performances at the Metropolitan Opera House and the New Theatre at the end of the season of 1909-10. One of her rôles was Rosina, which is a greater favourite with Spanish women singers than Carmen. Margarita d'Alvarez, a Peruvian contralto born in Liverpool, sang in Oscar Hammerstein's last Manhattan Opera House season, and is now well-known in London.

The winter of 1915-16 beheld the Spanish

blaze. Enrique Granados, one of the most distinguished of contemporary Spanish pianists and composers, a man who took a keen interest in the survival, and artistic use, of national forms, came to this country to assist at the production of his opera *Goyescas*, sung in Spanish at the Metropolitan Opera House for the first time anywhere, and was also heard several times here in his interpretative capacity as a pianist ; Pablo Casals, the Spanish 'cellist, gave frequent exhibitions of his finished art, as did Miguel Llobet, the guitar virtuoso ; La Argentina (Señora Paz of South America) exposed her ideas, somewhat classicized, of Spanish dances ; a Spanish soprano, Maria Barrientos, made her North American début and justified, in some measure, the extravagant reports which had been spread broadcast about her singing.* Finally the decree of Paris (still valid in spite of Paul Poiret's reported absence in the trenches) led all our womenfolk into the wearing of Spanish garments, the hip-hoops of the Velazquez period, the lace flounces of Goya's Duchess of Alba, and the mantillas, the combs, and the *accroche-cœurs* of Spain, Spain, Spain. . . . In addition one must mention Mme. Farrar's brilliant success, deserved in some degree, as Carmen, both in Bizet's opera and in a moving picture drama ; Miss Theda Bara's film appearance in the same

---

*To these should be added Juan Nadal, tenor with the Chicago Opera Company, José Mardones, bass, Hipolito Lazaro, tenor, and Rafael Diaz, tenor, with the Metropolitan Opera Company.

part, made with more atmospheric suggestion than Mme. Farrar's, even if less effective as an interpretation of the moods of the Spanish cigarette girl ; Mr. Charles Chaplin's eccentric burlesque of the same play ; the continued presence in New York of Andres de Segurola as an opera and concert singer ; Maria Gay, who gave some performances in *Carmen* and other operas ; and Lucrezia Bori, although she was unable to sing during the entire season owing to the unfortunate result of an operation on her vocal cords ; in Chicago, Miss Supervia appeared at the opera and Mme. Kutznezoff, the Russian, danced Spanish dances ; and at the New York Winter Garden, Isabel Rodriguez appeared in Spanish dances which quite transcended the surroundings and made that stage as atmospheric, for the few brief moments in which it was occupied by her really entrancing beauty, as a *maison de danse* in Seville. The tango, too, in somewhat modified form, continued to interest " ballroom dancers," danced to music provided in many instances by Señor Valverde, an indefatigable producer of popular tunes, some of which have a certain value as music, owing to their close allegiance to the folk-dances and songs of Spain. In the art-world there was a noticeable revival of interest in Goya and El Greco.

But if Mr. Gatti-Casazza, with the best intentions in the world, should desire to take advantage of any of this *réclame* by producing a series of

Spanish operas at the Metropolitan Opera House
—say four or five more—he would find himself
in difficulty. Where are they? Pedrell's *La
Celestina* has found many admirers. Camille Bellaigue in " Notes Brèves " recommends it warmly
to the director of the Opéra-Comique in Paris:
" Aussi bien, après tant de ' saisons ' russes,
italiennes, allemandes, pourquoi ne pas en avoir
une espagnole ? " . . . Manuel de Falla's *La
Vida Breve* was produced in Paris before it was
heard in Madrid. G. Jean-Aubry praises it
highly. . . . And José María Usandizaga's *Las
Golondrinas* has proved immensely popular in
Spain.

Pianists have not been slow to realize the value
and beauty of Spanish music which they have
placed on their programs, if not in profusion,
at least in no niggardly manner . . . but so far
as I know no Spanish music has yet been played
by the New York symphony societies, although
works of Granados, and possibly those of other
Spanish composers, have been heard elsewhere in
America. This neglect is not only lamentable:
it is stupid. Whether the music is good or bad,
interesting or dull, New York should be permitted
to hear some of it. I should suggest, to begin
with, Albéniz's *Catalonia*, Joaquín Turina's *La
Procesión del Rocio*, Conrado del Campo's *Divina
Comedia*, Pérez Casas's *Suite Murcienne*, and Manuel de Falla's *Noches en los Jardines de España*.
Of these I should prefer to hear the second and

last. Several of the operas of Isaac Albéniz have been performed in London, and in Brussels at the Théâtre de la Monnaie, but would they be liked here? There is Felipe Pedrell's monumental work, the trilogy, *Los Pireneos*, called by Edouard Lopez-Chavarri " the most important work for the theatre written in Spain "; and there is the aforementioned *La Dolores*. For the rest, one would have to search about among the zarzuelas; and would the Metropolitan Opera House be a suitable place for the production of this form of opera? It was doubtful, indeed, if the zarzuela could take root in any theatre in New York. But now that we have heard *The Land of Joy* it is certain that a group of zarzuelas, presented by a good company with a good orchestra in the Spanish fashion, would be greeted here with enthusiasm.

The truth is that in Spain Italian and German operas are much more popular than Spanish, the zarzuela always excepted. (This situation must be quite familiar to any American or Englishman, for neither in America nor in England has English opera any standing.) At Señor Arbós's series of concerts at the Royal Opera in Madrid one hears more Bach and Beethoven than Albéniz and Pedrell. There is a growing interest in music in Spain and there are indications that some day her composers may again take an important place with the musicians of other nationalities, a place they proudly held in the sixteenth and seventeenth centuries. However, no longer ago than 1894, we find Louis Lombard writing in his " Observations of a Musician " that harmony was not taught at the Conservatory of Malaga, and that at the closing exercises of the Conservatory of Barcelona he had heard a four-hand arrangement of the *Tannhäuser* march performed on ten pianos by forty hands ! Havelock Ellis (" The Soul of Spain ", 1909) affirms that a concert in Spain sets the audience to chattering. They have a savage love of noise, the Spanish, he says, which incites them to conversation. Albert Lavignac, in " Music and Musicians " (William Marchant's translation), says " We have left in the shade the Spanish school, which to say truth does not exist." But if one reads what Lavignac has to say about Musorgsky, one is likely to give little credence to such extravagant generalities as the one just quoted. The Musorgsky paragraph is a gem, and I am only too glad to insert it here for the sake of those who have not seen it : " A charming and fruitful melodist, who makes up for a lack of skill in harmonization by a daring, which is sometimes of doubtful taste ; has produced songs, piano music in small amount, and an opera, *Boris Godunoff*." In the report of the proceedings of the thirty-fourth session of the London Musical Association (1907-8) Dr. Thomas Lea Southgate is quoted as complaining to Sir George Grove because under " Schools of Composition " in the old edition of Grove's "Dictionary" the Spanish School was dismissed in twenty lines. Sir George, he says, replied, "Well, I gave it to Rockstro because nobody knows anything about Spanish music."—The bibliography of modern Spanish music is indeed indescribably meagre, although a good deal has been written in and out of Spain about the early religious composers of the Iberian peninsula.

These matters will be discussed in due course. In the meantime it has afforded me some amusement to put together a list (which may be of interest to both the casual reader and the student of music) of compositions suggested by Spain to composers of other nationalities. (This list is by no means complete. I have not attempted to include in it works which are not more or less familiar to the public of the present day; without boundaries it could easily be extended into a small volume.) The répertoire of the concert room and the opera house is streaked through and through with Spanish atmosphere and, on the whole, I should say, the best Spanish music has not been written by Spaniards, although most of it, like the best music written in Spain, is based primarily on the rhythm of folk-tunes, dances and songs. Of orchestral pieces I think I must put at the head of the list Chabrier's rhapsody, *España*, as colourful and rhythmic a combination of tone as the auditor of a symphony concert is often bidden to hear. It depends for its melody and rhythm on two Spanish dances, the jota, fast and fiery, and the malagueña, slow and sensuous. These are true Spanish tunes; Chabrier, according to report, invented only the rude theme given to the trombones. The piece was originally written for piano, and after Chabrier's death was transformed (with other music by the same composer) into a ballet, *España*, performed at the Paris Opéra, 1911. Waldteufel based one of his most popular waltzes on the theme of this rhapsody. Chabrier's *Habanera* for the pianoforte (1885) was his last musical reminiscence of his journey to Spain. It is French composers generally who have achieved better effects with Spanish atmosphere than men of other nations, and next to Chabrier's music I should put Debussy's *Iberia*, the second of his *Images* (1910). It contains three movements designated respectively as " In the streets and roads," " The perfumes of the night," and " The morning of a fête-day." It is indeed rather the smell and the look of Spain than the rhythm that this music gives us, entirely impressionistic that it is, but rhythm is not lacking, and such characteristic instruments as castanets, tambourines, and xylophones are required by the score. " Perfumes of the night " comes as near to suggesting odours to the nostrils as any music can—and not all of them are pleasant odours. There is Rimsky-Korsakoff's *Capriccio Espagnole*, with its *alborada* or lusty morning serenade, its long series of cadenzas (as cleverly written as those of *Scheherazade* to display the virtuosity of individual players in the orchestra ; it is noteworthy that this work is dedicated to the sixty-seven musicians of the band at the Imperial Opera House of Petrograd and all of their names are mentioned on the score) to suggest the vacillating music of a gipsy encampment, and finally the wild fandango of the Asturias with which the work comes to a brilliant conclusion. Engelbert Humperdinck taught the theory of music in the Conservatory of Barcelona for two years (1885-6), and one of the results was his *Maurische Rhapsodie* in three parts (1898-9), still occasionally performed by our orchestras. Lalo wrote his *Symphonie Espagnole* for violin and orchestra for the great Spanish virtuoso, Pablo de Sarasate, and all our violinists delight to perform it (although usually shorn of a movement or two). Glinka wrote a *Jota Aragonese* and *A Night in Madrid* ; he gave a Spanish theme to Balakireff which the latter utilized in his *Overture on a theme of a Spanish March*. Liszt wrote a *Spanish Rhapsody* for pianoforte (arranged as a concert piece for piano and orchestra by Busoni) in which he used the jota of Aragon as a theme for variations. Rubinstein's *Toreador and Andalusian* and Moszkowski's *Spanish Dances* (for four hands) are known to all amateur pianists, as Hugo Wolf's *Spanisches Liederbuch* and Robert Schumann's *Spanisches Liederspiel*, set to E.

Geibel's translations of popular Spanish ballads, are known to all singers. I have heard a song of Saint-Saëns, *Guitares et Mandolines*, charmingly sung by Greta Torpadie, in which the instruments of the title, under the subtle fingers of that masterly accompanist, Coenraad V. Bos, were cleverly imitated. And Debussy's *Mandoline* and Delibes's *Les Filles de Cadix* (which in America belongs both to Emma Calvé and Olive Fremstad) spring instantly to mind. Ravel's *Rapsodie Espagnole* is as Spanish as music could be. Ravel based the habanera section of his *Rapsodie* on one of his piano pieces. But Richard Strauss's two tone-poems on Spanish subjects, *Don Juan* and *Don Quixote*, have not a note of Spanish colouring, so far as I can remember, from beginning to end. Svendsen's symphonic poem, *Zorahayda*, based on a passage in Washington Irving's " Alhambra ", is Spanish in theme and may be added to this list together with Waldteufel's *Estudiantina* waltzes. Anton Rubinstein wrote a tone-poem with the title, *Don Quixote*. The second of Debussy's *Estampes* for piano, *La Soirée dans Grenade* should be mentioned. Pablo Casals ('cellist) and Ruth Deyo (pianist) played Loeffler's *Poème Espagnole* at a concert in Boston March 24, 1917.

Four modern operas stand out as Spanish in subject and atmosphere. I would put at the top of the list Zandonai's *Conchita* ; the Italian composer has caught on his musical palette and transferred to his tonal canvas a deal of the lazy restless colour of the Iberian peninsula in this little master-work. The feeling of the streets and patois is admirably caught. The critic of the "New York Globe," Pitts Sanborn, said of it, after its solitary performance at the Metropolitan Opera House in New York by the Chicago Opera Company, " There is musical atmosphere of a rare and penetrating kind ; there is colour used with the discretion of a master ; there are intoxicating rhythms, and above the orchestra the voices are heard in a truthful musical speech. . . . Ever since *Carmen* it has been so easy to write Spanish music and achieve supremely the banal. Here there is as little of the Spanish of convention as in Debussy's *Iberia*, but there is Spain." This opera, based on Pierre Louÿs's sadic novel, " La Femme et le Pantin ", owed some of its extraordinary impression of vitality to the vivid performance given of the title-rôle by Tarquinia Tarquini. Raoul Laparra, born in Bordeaux, who has travelled much in Spain, has written two Spanish operas, *La Habanera* and *La Jota*, both named after popular Spanish dances and both produced at the Opéra-Comique in Paris. I have heard *La Habanera* there and found the composer's use of the dance as a pivot of a tragedy very convincing. Nor shall I forget the first act-close, in which a young man, seated on a wall facing the window of a house where a most bloody murder has been committed, sings a

TARQUINIA TARQUINI AS CONCHITA
from a photograph by Matzene

wild Spanish ditty, accompanying himself on the guitar, crossing and recrossing his legs in complete abandonment to the rhythm, while in the house rises the wild treble cry of a frightened child. I have not heard *La Jota*, nor have I seen the score. I do not find Emile Vuillermoz enthusiastic in his review ("S. I. M.," May 15, 1911) : " Une danse transforme le premier acte en un kaléidoscope frénétique et le combat dans l'église doit donner, au second, dans l'intention de l'auteur ' une sensation à pic, un peu comme celle d'un puits où grouillerait la besogne monstreuse de larves humaines.' A vrai dire ces deux tableaux de cinématographe papillotant, corsés de cris, de hurlements et d'un nombre incalculable de coups de feu constituent pour le spectateur une épreuve physiquement douloureuse, une hallucination confusé et inquiétante, un cauchemar assourdissant qui le conduisent irrésistiblement à l'hébétude et à la migraine. Dans tout cet enfer que devient la musique ? " Perhaps opera-goers in general are not looking for thrills of this order ; the fact remains that *La Jota* has had a modest career when compared with *La Habanera*, which has even been performed in Boston. Raoul Laparra, who is of Basque blood, has been almost constantly obsessed with the idea of Spain and has probably written more consistently Spanish music than some Iberian composers who might be mentioned. There is to be another dance-opera, he writes me, to add to *La Habanera* and *La Jota*, to be called *Le Tango et la Malagueña*, thus completing the series of " three dramas suggested by dances." Mr. Laparra married an American and is at present living in America. He has completed an opera entitled *Le Conquistador*, which obviously has to do with the Spanish occupation of America. He has also written a book, " La Musique Populaire en Espagne" (Delagrave ; Paris). "The best Spanish composer *is* the people," is his phrase.

At a concert in Aeolian Hall, January 6, 1917, Harold Bauer played Laparra's *Rhythmes Espagnoles* (announced as the first performance in New York). These proved to be a series of characteristic dance impressions. The composer supplied the following comment :

"There exists a world in Spain, little known outside the Iberian peninsula itself, made up of these people with their schools, their traditions. That is what I have tried to seize, that is what I am passionately interested in. Without the use of native tunes I have moulded my music on the native rhythms and forms and thereby endeavoured to interpret the spirit of the people Thus *Petenera* is conceived in the characteristic style and rhythm created by the singer of that name, an Andalusian woman, who lived in the last century. Old singers who had heard her told me that she sang ' like an angel.' Nobody could tell the date of her birth or death, and she has become a legendary character for whom all

Andalusia wept and still weeps, although her beauty and her voice caused many men much unhappiness.

"*Tientos* reproduces the impression of those mysterious comments of the guitar before or during the singer's sobbing melodic figures. The singer and the guitar-player improvise together and, strangely enough, always in harmony, as though animated by a single impulse.

"The *Sevillanas* is authentic in form. Its four figures portray the dance. In the Sevillana two dancers, one in red, the other in yellow, chase each other like two big butterflies, amidst the rattle of the castanets. It is at once the most graceful and the *proudest* dance I know.

"*Rueda* is built up on the rhythm of the Castilian dance of that name in 5-8 time. We are no longer in Andalusia, but in another scene: high plateaus, where, grave as the natural surroundings, massive beings dance who seem to have come out of the past. It is a dance of dead cities, Avila, Burgos and many others sleeping in the sublime sadness of old Castile where the great winds weep.

"*Soleá* belongs to a world of magic, a world of gipsies. Each of these gipsies seems to have in his heart and in his eyes some grief, some unrecognized fatality. Hence the motive of my *Habanera* and the character of its hero, Ramon.

"*Paseo;* sun, copper, red, gold—such are the vibrations of sound and sight of the Spanish fête.

It is especially at the bull-fights that they dazzle you, when, amid the wild acclamations of an excited assembly the *Cuadrilla*—the troop of combatants and caparisoned horses and mules—makes its entry into the arena. Such is the subject of this musical ' note.' "

Mr. Laparra elaborated this suite, adding other piano pieces and songs, and on April 24, 1918, in Aeolian Hall, with the assistance of Helen Stanley, soprano, he gave a concert at Aeolian Hall, New York, which he entitled " A Musical Journey Through Spain." " They are not songs as they are sung in Spain," said Mr. Laparra, " but they are the musical forms of that country expressed through the vision of a French traveller and treated by him with complete imaginative freedom." Mr. Laparra was born May 13, 1876, and studied at the Paris Conservatoire with Massenet and Gabriel Fauré. He secured the Prix de Rome in 1903.

Carmen is essentially a French opera ; the leading emotions of the characters are expressed in an idiom as French as that of Gounod ; yet the dances and entr'actes are Spanish in colour. According to Mr. Sterling Mackinlay, Manuel Garcia, who attended the first performance of *Carmen* in London, June 22, 1878, was " astounded and delighted at the Spanish colour in the music." The story of Carmen's entrance song is worth retelling in Mr. Philip Hale's words (" Boston Symphony Orchestra Programme

Notes "; 1914-15, P. 287) : " Mme. Galli-Marié disliked her entrance air, which was in 6-8 time with a chorus. She wished something more audacious, a song in which she could bring into play the whole battery of her *perversités artistiques*, to borrow Charles Pigot's phrase : ' caressing tones and smiles, voluptuous inflections, killing glances, disturbing gestures.' During the rehearsals Bizet made a dozen versions. The singer was satisfied only with the thirteenth, the now familiar Habanera, based on an old Spanish tune that had been used by Sebastian Yradier. This brought Bizet into trouble, for Yradier's publisher, Heugel, demanded that the indebtedness should be acknowledged in Bizet's score. Yradier made no complaint, but to avoid a lawsuit or a scandal, Bizet gave consent, and on the first page of the Habanera in the French edition of *Carmen* this line is engraved : ' Imitated from a Spanish song, the property of the publishers of *Le Ménestrel*.' "

There are other operas the scenes of which are laid in Spain. Some of them make an attempt at Spanish colouring, more do not. Massenet wrote no less than five operas on Spanish subjects, *Le Cid*, *Chérubin*, *Don César de Bazan*, *La Navarraise* and *Don Quichotte* (Cervantes's novel has frequently lured the composers of lyric dramas with its story ; Clément et Larousse give a long list of *Don Quixote* operas, but they do not include one by Manuel Garcia, which is mentioned in John

Towers's compilation, " Dictionary-Catalogue of Operas." This opera is recorded, however, in Hugo Riemann's " Opern Handbuch " together with others on the same subject by Purcell, Paesiello, Salieri, and Piccinni. However, not a single one of these lyric dramas has held its place on the stage). The Spanish dances in *Le Cid* are frequently performed, although the opera is not. The most famous of the set is called simply *Aragonaise*; it is not a jota. *Pleurez, mes yeux*, the principal air of the piece, can scarcely be called Spanish. There is a delightful suggestion of the jota in *La Navarraise*. In *Don Quichotte* la belle Dulcinée sings one of her airs to her own guitar strummings, and much was made of the fact, before the original production at Monte Carlo, of Mme. Lucy Arbell's lessons on that instrument. Mary Garden, who had learned to dance for *Salome*, took no guitar lessons for *Don Quichotte*. But is not the guitar an anachronism in this opera ? In a pamphlet by Don Cecilio de Roda, issued during the celebration of the tercentenary of the publication of Cervantes's romance, taking as its subject the musical references in the work, I find, " The harp was the aristocratic instrument most favoured by women and it would appear to be regarded in *Don Quixote* as the feminine instrument par excellence." Was the guitar as we know it in existence at that epoch ? I think the *vihuela* was the guitar of the period. . . . Maurice Ravel wrote a Spanish opera, *l'Heure Espagnole* (one act, performed at the Paris Opéra-Comique, 1911). Octave Séré ("Musiciens français d'Aujourd'hui") says of it : " Les principaux traits de son caractère et l'influence du sol natal s'y combinent étrangement. De l'alliance de la mer et du Pays Basque (Ravel was born in the Basses-Pyrénées, near the sea) est née une musique à la fois fluide et nerveusement rythmée, mobile, chatoyante, amie du pittoresque et dont le trait net et précis est plus incisif que profond." Hugo Wolf's opera *Der Corregidor* is founded on the novel, " El Sombrero de tres Picos," of the Spanish writer, Pedro de Alarcón (1833-91).* His unfinished opera *Manuel Venegas* also has a Spanish subject, suggested by Alarcón's " El Niño de la Bola." Other Spanish operas are Beethoven's *Fidelio*, Balfe's *The Rose of Castile*, Verdi's *Ernani* and *Il Trovatore*,†

*This amusing novel of Alarcón, translated by Jacob S. Fassett, jr. has recently been published by Alfred A. Knopf.

†We are not accustomed to think of Verdi's opera as Spanish to-day. But read Henry Fothergill Chorley (" Thirty Years' Musical Recollections ") : " One of the points in *Il Trovatore*—which may be found worthy of remembering—after this or the other tune has passed into the limbo of old tunes—is Signor Verdi's essay at vocal Spanish gipsy colour. The chorus of waifs and strays opening the second act has an uncouthness,—a bar or two of Oriental drawl,—before the Italian anvils begin,—which must remind any one of such real gipsy music, as can be heard and seen in Spain.—Thus, also, is the monotonous, inexpressive narration of the gipsy mother, Azucena, to be animated only by her own passion,—all the more truthful (possibly) from its want of character. No melody really exists among those people,—and the wild cries which they give out could not be reduced to notation, were it not for the dance which they accompany.—Signor Verdi may have comprehended this—though with insufficient means of expression : at all events, some notion of the kind is to be found in what may be called the characteristic music of *Il Trovatore*."

Rossini's *Il Barbiere di Siviglia*, Mozart's *Don Giovanni* and *Le Nozze di Figaro*,* Weber's *Preciosa*† (really a play with incidental music). To this list of operas should be added Cherubini's *Les Abencérages*, Donizetti's *La Favorita*, Camille Erlanger's *La Sorcière*, Lecocq's *Giroflé Girofla*, Wallace's *Maritana*, d'Albert's *Tiefland*, Verdi's *Don Carlos* and *La Forza del Destino*, Sir Arthur Sullivan's *The Chieftain*, Julius Eichberg's *The Doctor of Alcantara*, and Dargomisky's *The Statue Guest* (Pushkin's version of the Don Juan story. This opera, by the way, was one of the many retouched and completed by Rimsky-Korsakoff), Reznicek's *Donna Diana*—and Wagner's *Parsifal*! The American composer John Knowles Paine's opera *Azara*, dealing with a Moorish subject, has, I think, never been performed.

---

*" With regard to *Don Giovanni* and *Le Nozze di Figaro* " : It is interesting to find Arthur Symons in " Cities " writing : " Seville, more than any city I have ever seen, is the city of pleasure . . . and in living gaily, and in the present, it is carrying on a tradition : it is the city of Don Juan, the city of Figaro."

†In 1820-21 Weber completed a sketch of the first act and a duet out of the second of *Die Drei Pintos*, a Spanish comic opera. A predilection for Spanish subjects is observable in Weber about this period and may be attributed to the influence of Tieck. Columbus, Pizarro, Don Juan of Austria, and the Cid, all passed before him as possible subjects for operas.

II

The early religious composers of Spain deserve a niche all to themselves, be it ever so tiny, as in the present instance. There is, to be sure, some doubt as to whether their inspiration was entirely peninsular, or whether some of it was wafted from Flanders, and the rest gleaned in Rome, for in their service to the church most of them migrated to Italy and did their best work there. It is not the purpose of the present chronicler to devote much space to these early men, or to discuss in detail their music. There are no books in English devoted to a study of Spanish music, and few in any language, but what few exist take good care to relate at considerable length (some of them with frequent musical quotation) the state of music in Spain in the sixteenth, seventeenth, and eighteenth centuries, the golden period. To the reader who may wish to pursue this phase of our subject I offer a small bibliography. There is first of all A. Soubies's two volumes, "Histoire de la Musique d'Espagne," published in 1889. The second volume takes us through the eighteenth century. The religious and early secular composers are catalogued in these volumes, but there is little attempt at detail, and he is a happy composer who is awarded an entire page. Soubies does not find occasion to pause for more than a paragraph on most of his subjects. Occasionally, however, he lightens the plodding progress of the reader, as when he quotes Father Bermudo's " Declaración de Instrumentos " (1548) : " There are three kinds of instruments in music. The first are called natural ; these are men, of whom the song is called *musical harmony*. Others are artificial and are played by the touch—such as the harp, the *vihuela* (the ancient guitar, which resembles the lute), and others like them ; the music of these is called *artificial* or rhythmic. The third species is pneumatique and includes instruments such as the flute, the douçaine (a species of oboe), and the organ." There may be some to dispute this ingenious and highly original classification. The best known, and perhaps the most useful (because it is easily accessible) history of Spanish music is that written by Mariano Soriano Fuertes, in four volumes : " Historia de la Música Española desde la venida de los Fenicios hasta el año de 1850 " ; published in Barcelona and Madrid in 1855. There is further the " Diccionario Técnico, Histórico, y Biográfico de la Música," by José Parada y Barreto (Madrid, 1867). This, of course, is a general work on music, but Spain gets her full due. For example, a page and a half is devoted to Beethoven, and nine pages to Eslava. It is to this latter composer to whom we must turn for the most complete and important work on Spanish church music : " Lira Sacro-Hispana " (Madrid, 1869), in ten volumes, with voluminous extracts from the composers' works. This collection of Spanish church music from the sixteenth century through the eighteenth, with biographical notices of the composers is out of print and rare. As a valuable complement to it I may mention Felipe Pedrell's " Hispaniae Schola Musica Sacra," begun in 1894 which has already reached the proportions of Eslava's work. Pedrell, who was the master of Enrique Granados, has also issued a fine edition of the music of Victoria. The latest book on the subject is H. E. Collet's " Le mysticisme musical espagnol au XVIe siècle " (Félix Alcan ; Paris). Collet has also written a life of Victoria.

The Spanish composers had their full share in the process of crystallizing music into forms of permanent beauty during the sixteenth and seventeenth centuries. Rockstro asserts that during the early part of the sixteenth century nearly all the best composers for the great Roman choirs were Spaniards. But their greatest achievement was the foundation of the school of which Palestrina was the crown. On the music of their own country their influence is less perceptible. I think the name of Cristóbal Morales (1512–53) is the first important name in the history of Spanish music. He preceded Palestrina in Rome and some of his masses and motets are still sung in the Papal chapel there (and in other Roman Catholic edifices and by choral societies). Francisco Guerrero (1528-99; these dates are approximate) was a pupil of Morales. He wrote settings of the Passion choruses according to St. Matthew and St. John and numerous masses and motets. Tomás Luis de Victoria is, of course, the greatest figure in Spanish music, and next to Palestrina (with whom he worked contemporaneously) the greatest figure in sixteenth century music. Soubies writes : " One might say that on his musical palette he has entirely at his disposition, in some sort, the glowing colour of Zurbaran, the realistic and transparent tones of Velazquez, the ideal shades of Juan de Juanes and Murillo. His mysticism is that of Santa Teresa and San Juan de la Cruz." The music of Victoria is still very much alive and the Roman choirs still sing it. . . .

The list might be extended indefinitely . . . but the great names I have given. There are Cabezón, whom Pedrell calls the " Spanish Bach," Navarro, Caseda, Gomez, Ribera, Castillo, Lobo, Durón, Romero, Juarez. On the whole I think these composers had more influence on Rome— the Spanish nature is more reverent than the Italian—than on Spain. The modern Spanish composers have learned more from the folk-song and dance than they have from the church composers. However, there are voices which dissent from this opinion. G. Tebaldini (" Rivista Musicale," Vol. IV, Pp. 267 and 494) says that Pedrell in his studies learned much which he turned to account in the choral writing of his operas. And Felipe Pedrell himself asserts that there is an unbroken chain between the religious composers of the sixteenth century and the theatrical composers of the seventeenth. We may follow him thus far without believing that the theatrical composers of the seventeenth century had too great an influence on the secular composers of the present day.

III

All the world dances in Spain, at least it would seem so, in reading over the books of the Marco Polos who have made voyages of discovery on the Iberian peninsula. Guitars seem to be as common there as pea-shooters in New England, and strumming seems to set the feet a-tapping and voices a-singing, what, they care not. (Havelock Ellis says : " It is not always agreeable to the Spaniard to find that dancing is regarded by the foreigner as a peculiar and important Spanish institution. Even Valera, with his wide culture, could not escape this feeling ; in a review of a book about Spain by an American author entitled ' The Land of the Castanet '—a book which he recognized as full of appreciation for Spain—Valera resented the title. It is, he says, as though a book about the United States should be called ' The Land of Bacon.' ") Oriental colour is streaked through and through the melodies and harmonies, many of which betray their Arabian origin ; others are *flamenco*, or gipsy. The dances, almost invariably accompanied by song, are generally in 3-4 time or its variants such as 6-8 or 3-8 ; the tango, of course, is in 2-4. But the dancers evolve the most elaborate inter-rhythms out of these simple measures, creating thereby a complexity of effect which defies any comprehensible notation on paper. As it is on this *fioritura*, if I may be permitted to use the word in this connection, of the dancer that the sophisticated composer bases some of his most natural and national effects, I shall linger on the subject. La Argentina has re-arranged many of the Spanish dances for purposes of the concert stage, but in her translation she has retained in a large measure this interesting complication of rhythm, marking the irregularity of the beat, now with a singularly complicated detonation of heel-tapping, now with a sudden bend of a knee, now with the subtle quiver of an eyelash, now with a shower of castanet sparks (an instrument which requires a hard tutelage for its complete mastery ; Richard Ford tells us that even the children in the streets of Spain rap shells together, to become self-taught artists in the use of it). Probably Pastora Imperio is the foremost of all contemporary Spanish dancers. She is a gipsy, the daughter of the dancer, La Mejorana, and Victor Rojas, a tailor to bull-fighters, and she married the *torero*, El Gallo. She made her début at the Japonés, the best variety theatre in Madrid, opened in 1900. In 1902 she went to the Novedadés in the Calle Alcalá, where La Argentina, then known as Aidá, and the famous Amalia Molina first appeared in Madrid. The Brothers Quintero have inscribed a sonnet to Pastora Imperio and they wrote their " Historia de Sevilla " for her use. Julio Romero de Torres has painted her. And Benavente, one of the best of modern Spanish writers, has written a description of her dancing : " Her flesh burns with the consuming heat of all eternity, but her body is like the very pillar of the sanctuary, palpitating as it is kindled in the glow of sacred fires. . . . Watching Pastora Imperio life becomes more intense. The loves and hates of other worlds pass before our eyes and we feel ourselves heroes, bandits, hermits assailed by temptation, shameless bullies of the tavern—whatever is highest and lowest in one. A desire to shout out horrible things takes possession of us: *Gitanaza!* Thief! Assassin! Then we turn to curse. Finally, summing it all up, in a burst of exaltation we praise God, because we believe in God while we look at Pastora Imperio, just as we do when we read Shakespeare." Recently La Imperio has been appearing in a one act piece, the music of which was arranged from de Falla's *El Amor Brujo*.

Amalia Molina, mentioned above, was in her prime ten years or so ago. . . . Zuloaga has painted several portraits of Anita Ramirez and other Spanish dancers. One of his most admired pictures is of a gipsy dancer in *torero* costume.

Here, too, I may speak of La Goya, a delightful music-hall singer who has won fame not only in Spain but in South America as well. She has made a special study of costumes. Of a more popular type, but not more of a favourite, is Raquel Meller. Chabrier, in his visit to Spain with his wife in 1882, attempted to note down some of the rhythmic variations achieved by the dancers while the musicians strummed their

LA ARGENTINA
from a photograph by White

guitars, and he was partially successful. But all in all he only succeeded in giving in a single measure each variation; he did not attempt to weave them into the intricate pattern which the Spanish women contrive to make of them.

There is a singular similarity to be observed between this heel-tapping and the complicated drum-tapping of the African negroes of certain tribes. In his book " Afro-American Folksongs " H. E. Krehbiel thus describes the musical accompaniment of the dances in the Dahoman Village at the World's Columbian Exposition in Chicago: " These dances were accompanied by choral song and the rhythmical and harmonious beating of drums and bells, the song being in unison. The harmony was a tonic major triad broken up rhythmically in a most intricate and amazingly ingenious manner. The instruments were tuned with excellent justness. The fundamental tone came from a drum made of a hollowed log about three feet long with a single head, played by one who seemed to be the leader of the band, though there was no giving of signals. This drum was beaten with the palms of the hands. A variety of smaller drums, some with one, some with two heads, were beaten variously with sticks and fingers. The bells, four in number, were of iron and were held mouth upward and struck with sticks. The players showed the most remarkable rhythmical sense and skill that ever came under my notice. Berlioz in his supremest effort with his army of drummers produced nothing to compare in artistic interest with the harmonious drumming of these savages. The fundamental effect was a combination of double and triple time, the former kept by the singers, the latter by the drummers, but it is impossible to convey the idea of the wealth of detail achieved by the drummers by means of exchange of the rhythms, syncopation of both simultaneously, and dynamic devices. Only by making a score of the music could this have been done. I attempted to make such a score by enlisting the help of the late John C. Filmore, experienced in Indian music, but we were thwarted by the players who, evidently divining our purpose when we took out our notebooks, mischievously changed their manner of playing as soon as we touched pencil to paper."

The resemblance between negro and Spanish music is very noticeable. Mr. Krehbiel says that in South America Spanish melody has been imposed on negro rhythm. In the dances of the people of Spain, as Chabrier points out, the melody is often practically nil; the effect is rhythmic (an effect which is emphasized by the obvious harmonic and melodic limitations of the guitar, which invariably accompanies all singers and dancers). If there were a melody or if the guitarists played well (which they usually do not) one could not distinguish its contours what with the cries of " Ole !" and the heel-beats of the performers. Spanish melodies, indeed, are often scraps of tunes, like the African negro melodies. The habanera is a true African dance, taken to Spain by way of Cuba, as Albert Friedenthal points out in his book, " Musik, Tanz, und Dichtung bei den Kreolen Amerikas." Whoever was responsible, Arab, negro, or Moor (Havelock Ellis says that the dances of Spain are closely allied with the ancient dances of Greece and Egypt), the Spanish dances betray their oriental origin in their complexity of rhythm (a complexity not at all obvious on the printed page, as so much of it depends on dancer, guitarist, singer, and even public !), and the *fioriture* which decorate their melody when melody occurs. While Spanish religious music is perhaps not distinctively Spanish, the dances invariably display marked national characteristics ; it is on these, then (some in greater, some in less degree), that the composers in and out of Spain have built their most atmospheric inspirations, their best pictures of popular life in the Iberian peninsula. A good deal of the interest of this music is due to the important part the guitar plays in its construction ; the modulations are often contrary to all rules of harmony and (yet, some would say) the music seems to be effervescent with variety and fire. Of the guitarists Richard Ford (" Gatherings from Spain ") says : " The performers seldom are very scientific musicians ; they content themselves with striking the chords, sweeping the whole hand over the strings, or flourishing, and tapping the board with the thumb, at which they are very expert. Occasionally in the towns there is some one who has attained more power over this ungrateful instrument; but the attempt is a failure. The guitar responds coldly to Italian words and elaborate melody, which never come home to Spanish ears or hearts." An exception must be made in the case of Miguel Llobet. I first heard him play at Pitts Sanborn's concert at the Punch and Judy Theatre (April 17, 1916) for the benefit of Hospital 28 in Bourges, France, and he made a deep impression on me. In one of his numbers, the *Spanish Fantasy* of Tarrega, he astounded and thrilled me. He seemed at all times to exceed the capacity of his instrument, obtaining a variety of colour which was truly amazing. In this particular number he not only plucked the keyboard but the fingerboard as well, in intricate and rapid *tempo*; seemingly two different kinds of instruments were playing. But at all times he varied his tone; sometimes he made the instrument sound almost as though it had been played by wind and not plucked. Especially did I note a suggestion of the bagpipe. A true artist. None of the music, the fantasy mentioned, a serenade of Albéniz, and a Menuet of Sor, was particularly interesting, although the Fantasia contained some fascinating references to folk-dance tunes.

The Spanish dances are infinite in number and for centuries back they seem to form part and parcel of Spanish life. Discussion as to how they are danced is a feature of the descriptions. No two authors agree, it would seem; to a mere annotator the fact is evident that they are danced differently on different occasions. It is obvious that they are danced differently in different provinces. The Spaniards, as Richard Ford points out, are not too willing to give information to strangers, frequently because they themselves lack the knowledge. Their statements are often misleading, sometimes intentionally so. They do not understand the historical temperament. Until recently many of the art treasures and archives of the peninsula were but poorly kept. Those who lived in the shadow of the Alhambra admired only its shade. It may be imagined that there has been even less interest displayed in recording the folk-dances. "Dancing in Spain is now a matter which few know anything about," writes Havelock Ellis, "because every one takes it for granted that he knows all about it; and any question on the subject receives a very ready answer which is usually of questionable correctness." Of the music of the dances we have many records, and that they are generally in 3-4 time or its variants we may be certain. As to whether they are danced by two women, a woman and a man, or a woman alone, the authorities do not always agree. The confusion is added to by the oracular attitude of the scribes. It seems quite certain to me that this procedure varies. That the animated picture almost invariably possesses great fascination there are only too many witnesses to prove. I myself can testify to the marvel of some of them, set to be sure in strange frames, the Feria in Paris, for example; but even without the surroundings, which Spanish dances demand, the diablerie, the shivering intensity of these fleshly women, always wound tight with such shawls as only the mistresses of kings might wear in other countries, have drawn taut the *real thrill*. It is dancing which enlists the cooperation not only of the feet and legs, but of the arms and, in fact, the entire body.

The smart world in Spain to-day dances much as the smart world does anywhere else, although it does not, I am told, hold a brief for our tango, which Mr. Krehbiel suggests is a corruption of the original African habanera. But in older days many of the dances, such as the pavana, the sarabande, and the gallarda, were danced at the court and were in favour with the nobility. (Although presumably of Italian origin, the pavana and gallarda were more popular in Spain than in Rome. Fuertes says that the sarabande was invented in the middle of the sixteenth century by a dancer called Zarabanda who was a native of either Seville or Guayaquil.) The pavana, an ancient dance of grave and stately measure, was much in vogue in the sixteenth and seventeenth centuries. An explanation of its name is that the figures executed by the dancers bore a resemblance to the semi-circular wheel-like spreading of the tail of a peacock. In Catulle Mendès's song, *La Pavana*, set to music by Alfred Bruneau, he compares the pavane to a peacock. The gallarda (French, gaillard) was usually danced as a relief to the pavana (and indeed often follows it in the dance-suites of the classical composers in which these forms all figure). The jacara, or more properly xacara, of the sixteenth century, was danced in accompaniment to a romantic, swashbuckling ditty. The Spanish folias were a set of dances danced to a simple tune treated in a variety of styles with very free accompaniment of castanets and bursts of song. Corelli in Rome in 1700 published twenty-four variations in this form, which are often played in our day by violinists.

The names of the modern Spanish dances are often confused in the descriptions offered by observing travellers, for the reasons already noted. Hundreds of these descriptions exist, and it is difficult to choose the most telling of them. Gertrude Stein, who has spent the last two years in Spain, has noted the rhythm of several of these dances by the mingling of her original use of words with the ingratiating medium of *vers libre*. She has succeeded, I think, better than some musicians in suggesting the intricacies of the rhythm. I should like to transcribe one of these attempts here, but that I have not the right to do as I have only seen them in manuscript; they have not yet appeared in print. These pieces are in a sense the thing itself—I shall have to fall back on descriptions of the thing. The tirana, a dance common to the province of Andalusia, is accompanied by song. It has a decided rhythm, affording opportunities for grace and gesture, the women toying with their aprons, the men flourishing hats and handkerchiefs. The polo, or ole, is now a gipsy dance. Mr. Ellis asserts that it is a corruption of the sarabande! He goes on to say, " The so-called gipsy dances of Spain are Spanish dances which the Spaniards are tending to relinquish but which the gipsies have taken up with energy and skill." There have been adherents for the originality of the gipsy in the past, notably Liszt, but Salillas in his " Hampa " seems to have settled the matter once for all. The bolero, a comparatively modern dance, came to Spain through Italy. Mr. Philip Hale points out the fact that the bolero and the cachucha (which, by the way, one seldom hears of nowadays) were the popular Spanish dances when Mesdames Faviani and Dolores Tesrai, and their followers, Mlle. Noblet and Fanny Elssler, visited Paris. Fanny Elssler indeed is most frequently seen pictured in Spanish costume, and the cachucha was danced by her as often, I fancy, as Mme. Pavlova dances *Le Cygne* of Saint-Saëns. Marie-Anne de Camargo, who acquired great fame as a dancer in France in the early eighteenth century, was born in Brussels but was of Spanish descent. She relied, however, on the Italian classic style for her success rather than on national Spanish dances. The seguidilla is a gipsy dance which has the same rhythm as the bolero but is more animated and stirring. Examples of these dances, and of the jota, fandango, and the sevillana, are to be met with in the compositions listed in the first section of this article, in the appendices of Soriano Fuertes's " History of Spanish Music," in Grove's Dictionary, in the numbers of " S. I. M." in which the letters of Emmanuel Chabrier occur, and in collections made by P. Lacome, published in Paris.

The jota is another dance in 3-4 time. Every province in Spain has its own jota, but the most famous variations are those of Aragon, Valencia, and Navarre. It is accompanied by the guitar, the *bandurria* (similar to the guitar), small drum, castanets, and triangle. Mr. Hale says that its origin in the twelfth century[*] is attributed to a Moor named Alben Jot who fled from Valencia to Aragon. " The jota," he continues, " is danced not only at merrymakings but at certain religious festivals and even in watching the dead. One called the ' Natividad del Señor ' (nativity of our Lord) is danced on Christmas eve in Aragon, and is accompanied by songs, and jotas are sung and danced at the crossroads, invoking the favour of the Virgin, when the festival of Our Lady del Pilar is celebrated at Saragossa."

[*]Tomás Bretón writes me that he considers it ridiculous to attribute any such age to the jota. His researches on the subject are embodied in a pamphlet (1911) entitled " Rápida ojeada histórica sobre la música española."

Havelock Ellis's description of the jota is worth reproducing: "The Aragonaise jota, the most important and typical dance outside Andalusia, is danced by a man and a woman, and is a kind of combat between them; most of the time they are facing each other, both using castanets and advancing and retreating in an apparently aggressive manner, the arms alternately slightly raised and lowered, and the legs, with a seeming attempt to trip the partner, kicking out alternately somewhat sidewise, as the body is rapidly supported first on one side and then on the other. It is a monotonous dance, with immense rapidity and vivacity in its monotony, but it has not the deliberate grace and fascination, the happy audacities of Andalusian dancing. There is, indeed, no faintest suggestion of voluptuousness in it, but it may rather be said, in the words of a modern poet, Salvador Rueda, to have in it 'the sound of helmets and plumes and lances and banners, the roaring of cannon, the neighing of horses, the shock of swords.'"

Chabrier, in his astounding and amusing letters from Spain, gives us vivid pictures and interesting information. This one, written to his friend, Edouard Moullé, from Granada, November 4, 1882, appeared in "S. I. M." April 15, 1911 (I have omitted the musical illustrations, which, however, possess great value for the student): "In a month I must leave adorable Spain . . . and say good-bye to the Spaniards,—because, I say this only to you, they are very nice, the little girls! I have not seen a really ugly woman since I have been in Andalusia : I do not speak of the feet, they are so small that I have never seen them ; the hands are tiny and well-kept and the arms of an exquisite contour ; I speak only of what one can see, but they show a good deal ; add the arabesques, the side-curls, and other ingenuities of the coiffure, the inevitable fan, the flower and the comb in the hair, placed well behind, the shawl of Chinese crêpe, with long fringe and embroidered in flowers, knotted around the figure, the arm bare, and the eye protected by eyelashes which are long enough to curl ; the skin of dull white or orange colour, according to the race, all this smiling, gesticulating, dancing, drinking, and careless to the last degree. . . .

" That is the Andalusian.

" Every evening we go with Alice to the café-concerts where the malagueñas, the Soledas, the Sapatcados, and the Peteneras are sung ; then the dances, absolutely Arab, to speak truth ; if you could see them wriggle, unjoint their hips, contortion, I believe you would not try to get away ! . . At Malaga the dancing became so intense that I was compelled to take my wife away ; it wasn't even amusing any more. I can't write about it, but I remember it and I will describe it to you.— I have no need to tell you that I have noted down many things ; the tango, a kind of dance in which the women imitate the pitching of a ship (*le tangage du navire*) is the only dance in 2 time ; all the others, all, are in 3-4 (Seville) or in 3-8 (Malaga and Cadiz) ;—in the North it is different, there is some music in 5-8, very curious. The 2-4 of the tango is always like the habanera ; this is the picture : one or two women dance, two silly men play it doesn't matter what on their guitars, and five or six women howl, with excruciating voices and in triplet figures impossible to note down because they change the air—every instant a new scrap of tune. They howl a series of figurations with syllables, words, rising voices, clapping hands which strike the six quavers, emphasizing the third and the sixth, cries of Anda ! Anda ! La Salud ! eso es la Mariquita ! gracia ! Baila, la chiquilla ! Anda ! Anda ! Consuelo ! Olé, la Lola, olè la Carmen ! que gracia ! que elegancia ! all that to excite the young dancer. It is vertiginous—it is unspeakable!

"The Sevillana is another thing : it is in 3-4 time (and with castanets). . . . All this becomes extraordinarily alluring with two curls, a pair of castanets and a guitar. It is impossible to write down the malagueña. It is a melopœia, however, which has a form and which always ends on the dominant, to which the guitar furnishes 3-8 time, and the spectator (when there is one) seated beside the guitarist, holds a cane between his legs and beats the syncopated rhythm ; the dancers themselves instinctively syncopate the measures in a thousand ways, striking with their heels an unbelievable number of rhythms. . . . It is all rhythm and dance: the airs scraped out by the guitarist have no value; besides, they cannot be heard on account of the cries of Anda! la chiquilla! que gracia! que elegancia! Anda! Olè! Olè! la chiquirritita! and the more the cries the more the dancer laughs with her mouth wide open, and turns her hips, and is mad with her body. . . ." Curiously enough in a music critic's account of a voyage in Spain (H. T. Finck's "Spain and Morocco") only a single page is devoted to a discussion of Spanish music or dancing. The author is not sympathetic. The rhythmic and dynamic features of the performance which so aroused the delight of Chabrier only annoy Mr. Finck. I quote his account which begins with an experience at Murcia: "In the evening I came across an interesting performance in the street. A woman and a man were singing a duet, accompanying themselves with a guitar and a mandolin, making a peculiarly pleasing combination, infinitely superior to the performances of the Italian bards who accompany themselves with hand-organs or cheap harps, not to speak of the horrible German beer-bands which infest our streets. It was indeed so agreeable that I followed the couple for several blocks. But with the exception of a students' concert in Seville, it was almost the only good music I heard in Spain. Madrid and Barcelona have ambitious operatic performances in winter, and the Barcelonese go so far as to claim that they sing and understand Wagner better than the Berliners; but as the opera-houses were closed while I was there, I have no comments to offer on this boast. In a café chantant which I visited in Seville I heard, instead of national airs, vulgar French women singing a French version of 'Champagne Charley' and similar vulgar things; no one, it is true, cared for these songs, whereas a rare bit of national melody in the program was wildly applauded; but fashion of course must have her sway. At another café the music was thoroughly Spanish, with guitar accompaniment; but, according to the usual Spanish custom, there were a dozen persons on the stage who clapped their hands so loudly, to mark the rhythm, that the music degenerated into a mere rhythmic noise accompanying the dancing. These dances interest the Spanish populace much more than any kind of music, and I was amused occasionally to see a group of working men looking on the grotesque amateur dancing of one or two of their number with an expression of supreme enjoyment, and clapping their hands in unison to keep time."

Seeing indifferent dancing performed, he affirms, by women who were no longer young, in the early part of his Spanish sojourn, Théophile Gautier, too, at first was inclined to treat Spanish dancing as a myth: "Les danses espagnoles n'existent qu'à Paris, comme les coquillages, qu'on ne trouve que chez les marchands de

curiosités, et jamais sur le bord de la mer. O
Fanny Elssler ! qui êtes maintenant en Amérique
chez les sauvages, même avant d'aller en Espagne,
nous nous doutions bien que c'était vous qui aviez
inventé la cachucha ! " . . . This was at Vitoria.
In Madrid he writes : " On nous avait dit à Vitoria, à Burgos et à Valladolid, que les bonnes
danseuses étaient à Madrid ; à Madrid, l'on nous
a dit que les véritables danseuses de cachucha
n'existaient qu'en Andalousie, à Seville. Nous
verrons bien ; mais nous avons peur qu'en fait de
danses espagnoles, il ne nous faille en revenir à
Fanny Elssler et aux deux soeurs Noblet." . . .
In Andalusia he capitulated : " Les danseuses
espagnoles, bien qu'elles n'aient pas le fini, la cor-
rection précise, l'élévation des danseuses fran-
çaises, leur sont, à mon avis, bien supérieures par
la grâce et le charme ; comme elles travaillent peu
et ne s'assujetissent pas à ces terribles exercises
d'assouplissement qui font ressembler une classe
de danse à une salle de torture, elles évitent cette
maigreur de cheval entrainé qui donne à nos bal-
lets quelque chose de trop macabre et de trop
anatomique ; elles conservent les contours et les
rondeurs de leur sexe ; elles ont l'air de femmes
qui dansent et non pas de danseuses, ce qui est
bien différent. . . . En Espagne les pieds quittent
à peine la terre ; point de ces grands ronds de
jambe, de ces écarts qui font ressembler une
femme à un compas forcé, et qu'on trouve là-bas
d'une indécence révoltante. C'est le corps qui

danse, ce sont les reins qui se cambrent, les flancs qui ploient, la taille qui se tord avec une souplesse d'almée ou de couleuvre. Dans les poses renversées, les epaules de la danseuse vont presque toucher la terre ; les bras, pâmés et morts, ont une flexibilité, une mollesse d'écharpe dénouée ; on dirait que les mains peuvent à peine soulever et faire babiller les castagnettes d'ivoire aux cordons tressés d'or ; et cependant, au moment venu, des bonds de jeune jaguar succèdent à cette langueur voluptueuse, et prouvent que ces corps, doux comme la soie, enveloppent des muscles d'acier. . . . ." Gautier thus describes the malagueña : "La *malagueña*, danse locale de Malaga, est vraiment d'une poésie charmante. Le cavalier paraît d'abord, le *sombrero* sur les yeux, embossé dans sa cape écarlate comme un hidalgo qui se promène et cherche les aventures. La dame entre, drapée dans sa mantille, son éventail à la main, avec les façons d'une femme qui va faire un tour à l'Alameda. Le cavalier tâche de voir la figure de cette mystérieuse sirène ; mais la coquette manœuvre si bien de l'éventail, l'ouvre et le ferme si à propos, le tourne et le retourne si promptement à la hauteur de son joli visage, que le galant, désappointé, recule de quelques pas et s'avise d'un autre stratagème. Il fait parler des castagnettes sous son manteau. A ce bruit, la dame prête l'oreille ; elle sourit, son sein palpite, la pointe de son petit pied de satin marque la mesure malgré elle ; elle jette son éventail, sa mantille, et paraît en folle toilette de danseuse, étincelante de paillettes et de clinquants, une rose dans les cheveux, un grand peigne d'écaille sur la tête. Le cavalier se débarrasse de son masque et de sa cape, et tous deux exécutent un pas d'une originalité délicieuse."

As it is on these dances that composers invariably base their Spanish music (not alone Albéniz, Chapí, Bretón, and Granados, but Chabrier, Ravel, Laparra, and Bizet, as well) we may linger somewhat longer on their delights. The following compelling description is from Richard Ford's highly readable "Gatherings from Spain":
"The dance which is closely analogous to the *Ghowasee* of the Egyptians, and the *Nautch* of the Hindoos, is called the *Ole* by Spaniards, the *Romalis* by their gipsies; the soul and essence of it consists in the expression of a certain sentiment, one not indeed of a very sentimental or correct character. The ladies, who seem to have no bones, resolve the problem of perpetual motion, their feet having comparatively a sinecure, as the whole person performs a pantomime, and trembles like an aspen leaf; the flexible form and Terpsichore figure of a young Andalusian girl—be she gipsy or not—is said, by the learned, to have been designed by nature as the fit frame for her voluptuous imagination.

"Be that as it may, the scholar and classical commentator will every moment quote Martial, etc., when he beholds the unchanged balancing of hands, raised as if to catch showers of roses, the tapping of the feet, and the serpentine quivering movements. A contagious excitement seizes the spectators, who, like Orientals, beat time with their hands in measured cadence, and at every pause applaud with cries and clappings. The damsels, thus encouraged, continue in violent action until nature is all but exhausted; then aniseed brandy, wine, and *alpisteras* are handed about, and the fête, carried on to early dawn, often concludes in broken heads, which here are called 'gipsy's fare.' These dances appear, to a stranger from the chilly north, to be more marked by energy than by grace, nor have the legs less to do than the body, hips, and arms. The sight of this unchanged pastime of antiquity, which excites the Spaniard to frenzy, rather disgusts an English spectator, possibly from some national malorganization, for, as Molière says, ' l'Angleterre a produit des grands hommes dans les sciences et les beaux arts, mais pas un grand danseur—allez lire l'histoire.' " (A fact as true in our day as it was in Molière's.)

Arthur Symons has written a very beautiful passage to describe a gipsy dancing. If you have seen Doloretes you may think of her while you read it: " All Spanish dancing, and especially the dancing of the gipsies, in which it is seen in its most characteristic development, has a sexual origin, and expresses, as Eastern dancing does, but less crudely, the pantomime of physical love.

In the typical gipsy dance as I saw it danced by a beautiful Gitana at Seville, there is something of mere gaminerie and something of the devil; the automatic tramp-tramp of the children and the lascivious pantomime of a very learned art of love. Thus it has all the excitement of something spontaneous and studied, of vice and a kind of naughty innocence, of the thoughtless gaiety of youth as well as the knowing humour of experience. For it is a dance full of humour, fuller of humour than of passion; passion indeed it mimics on the purely animal side, and with a sort of coldness even in its frenzy. It is capable of infinite variations; it is a drama, but a drama improvised on a given theme; and it might go on indefinitely, for it is conditioned only by the pantomime which we know to have wide limits. A motion more or less and it becomes obscene or innocent; it is always on a doubtful verge, and thus gains its extraordinary fascination. I held my breath as I watched the gipsy in the Seville dancing-hall; I felt myself swaying unconsciously to the rhythm of her body, of her beckoning hands, of the glittering smile that came and went in her eyes. I seemed to be drawn into a shining whirlpool, in which I turned, turned, hearing the buzz of water settling over my head. The guitar buzzed, buzzed, in a prancing rhythm, the gipsy coiled about the floor, in her trailing dress, never so much as showing her ankles, with a rapidity concentrated upon itself; her hands beckoned, reached out, clutched delicately, lived to their finger-tips ; her body straightened, bent, the knees bent and straightened, the heels beat on the floor, carrying her backwards and round ; the toes pointed, paused, pointed, and the body drooped or rose into immobility, a smiling, significant pause of the whole body. Then the motion became again more vivid, more restrained, as if teased by some unseen limits, as if turning upon itself in the vain desire of escape, as if caught in its own toils ; more feverish, more fatal, the humour turning painful, with the pain of achieved desire ; more earnest, more eager, with the languor in which desire dies triumphant."

On certain days the sevillana is danced before the high altar of the cathedral at Seville. The Reverend Henry Cart de Lafontaine (" Proceedings of the Musical Association " ; London, thirty-third session, 1906-7) gives the following account of it, quoting a " French author " : " While Louis XIII was reigning over France, the Pope heard much talk of the Spanish dance called the ' Sevillana.' He wished to satisfy himself, by actual eye-witness, as to the character of this dance, and expressed his wish to a bishop of the diocese of Seville, who every year visited Rome. Evil tongues make the bishop responsible for the primary suggestion of the idea. Be that as it may, the bishop, on his return to Seville, had twelve youths well instructed in all the intricate measures of this Andalusian dance. He had to choose youths, for how could he present maidens to the horrified glance of the Holy Father? When his little troop was thoroughly schooled and perfected, he took the party to Rome, and the audience was arranged. The 'Sevillana' was danced in one of the rooms of the Vatican. The Pope warmly complimented the young executants, who were dressed in beautiful silk costumes of the period. The bishop humbly asked for permission to perform this dance at certain fêtes in the cathedral church at Seville, and further pleaded for a restriction of this privilege to that church alone. The Pope, hoist by his own petard, did not like to refuse, but granted the privilege with this restriction, that it should only last so long as the costumes of the dancers were wearable. Needless to say, these costumes are, therefore, objects of constant repair, but they are supposed to retain their identity even to this day. And this is the reason why the twelve boys who dance the 'Sevillana' before the high altar in the cathedral on certain feast days are dressed in the costume belonging to the reign of Louis XIII."

This is a very pretty story, but it is not uncontradicted. . . . Has any statement been made about Spanish dancing or music which has been allowed to go uncontradicted? Look upon that picture and upon this: "As far as it is possible to ascertain from records," says Rhoda G. Edwards in the "Musical Standard," "this dance would seem always to have been in use in Seville cathedral; when the town was taken from the Moors in the thirteenth century it was undoubtedly an established custom and in 1428 we find the six boys recognized as an integral part of the chapter by Pope Eugenius IV. The dance is known as the (*sic*) ' Los Seises,' or dance of the six boys who, with four others, dance it before the high altar at Benediction on the three evenings before Lent and in the octaves of Corpus Christi and La Purisima (the conception of Our Lady). The dress of the boys is most picturesque, page costumes of the time of Philip III being worn, blue for La Purisima and red satin doublets slashed with blue for the other occasion; white hats with blue and white feathers are also worn whilst dancing. The dance is usually of twenty-five minutes' duration and in form seems quite unique, not resembling any of the other Spanish dance-forms, or in fact those of any other country. The boys accompany the symphony on castanets and sing a hymn in two parts whilst dancing."

Another account of this dance in the cathedral may be found in de Amicis's " Spain and the Spaniards." . . . H. T. Finck saw this dance and he devotes a short paragraph to it on P. 56 of his " Spain and Morocco." Arthur Symons's description in his essay on " Seville " in " Cities " is charming enough to quote : " There was but little light except about the altar, which blazed with candles; suddenly a curtain was drawn aside, and the sixteen boys, in their blue and white

costume, holding plumed hats in their hands,
came forward and knelt before the altar. The
priests, who had been chanting, came up from the
choir; the boys rose, and formed in two eights,
facing each other, in front of the altar, and the
priests knelt in a semi-circle around them. Then
an unseen orchestra began to play, and the boys
put on their hats, and began to sing the *coplas* in
honour of the Virgin:

> ' O mi, O mi amada
> Immaculada!'

to a dance measure. And then after they had
sung the *coplas* they began to dance, still singing.
It was a kind of solemn minuet, the feet never
taken from the ground, a minuet of delicate step-
ping and intricate movement, in which a central
square would form, divide, a whole line passing
through the opposite line, the outer ends then re-
peating one another's movements while the others
turned and divided again in the middle. The first
movement was very slow, the second faster, end-
ing with a pirouette; then came two movements
without singing, but with the accompaniment of
castanets, the first movement again very slow, the
second a quick rattle of the castanets, like the
rattling of kettle-drums, but done without raising
the hands above the level of the elbows. Then
the whole thing was repeated from the beginning,
the boys flourished off their hats, dropped on their
knees before the altar, and went quickly out.

One or two verses were chanted, the Archbishop gave his benediction, and the ceremony was over.

"And, yes, I found it perfectly dignified, perfectly religious, without a suspicion of levity or indecorum. This consecration of the dance, this turning of a possible vice into a means of devotion, this bringing of the people's art, the people's passion, which in Seville is dancing, into the church, finding it a place there, is precisely one of those acts of divine wordly wisdom which the Church has so often practised in her conquest of the world."

From another author we learn that religious dancing is to be seen elsewhere in Spain than at Seville cathedral. At one time, it is said to have been common. The pilgrims to the shrine of the Virgin at Montserrat were wont to dance, and dancing took place in the churches of Valencia, Toledo, and Jerez. Religious dancing continued to be common, especially in Cataluña up to the seventeeth century. An account of the dance in the Seville cathedral may be found in "Los Españoles Pintados por si mismos" (pages 287-91).

This very incomplete and rambling record of Spanish dancing should include some mention of the fandango. The origin of the word is obscure, but the dance is obviously one of the gayest and wildest of the Spanish dances. Like the malagueña it is in 3-8 time, but it is quite different in spirit from that senuous form of terpsichorean enjoyment. La Argentina informs me

that " fandango " in Spanish suggests very much
what " bacchanale " does in English or French.
It is a very old dance, and may be a survival of a
Moorish dance, as Desrat suggests. Mr. Philip Hale
found the following account of it somewhere : *
" Like an electric shock, the notes of the
fandango animate all hearts. Men and women,
young and old, acknowledge the power of this air
over the ears and soul of every Spaniard. The
young men spring to their places, rattling cas-
canets, or imitating their sound by snapping their
fingers. The girls are remarkable for the wil-
lowy languor and lightness of their movements,
the voluptuousness of their attitudes—beating
the exactest time with tapping heels. Partners

*In the anonymous, incomplete, and somewhat incorrect translation
of Gaston Vuillier's " La Danse " (Hachette et Cie., 1898). In the
original work this description of the fandango seems to be attributed
to Tomás de Iriarte although the text is a little ambiguous. In the
English translation called, " A History of Dancing," Chapter VIII is
mainly devoted to Spanish dancing ; in the original work it is Chapter
IX. Vuillier derived most of his material for this chapter from the
Baron Charles Davillier's elaborate work, " l'Espagne," which is illustrated by Gustave Doré. Vuillier quotes Davillier very freely. Davil
lier's chapters on Spanish dancing (Chapters XIV and XV) are extremely
interesting and much of their material the Baron gathered himself.
There is for example a description of La Campanera dancing to the
indifferent music provided by a blind violinist whose tunes prove so
uninspiring that Doré seizes the violin from his trembling old fingers
and plays it himself with great effect. Davillier describes Doré as a
violinist of the first order who had won praise from Rossini. On
another occasion Davillier and Doré, stimulated by the dancing of
gipsies, enter into the sport themselves, wildly tap their heels, wave
their arms, and circle with the gitanas while a large group applauds.
This book, which was published by Hachette in Paris in 1874, was
brought out in New York, in J. Thomson's translation, with the original
illustrations, by Scribner, Welford, and Armstrong in 1876. In the
American edition the two French chapters are rolled into one, Chap. XIV.

tease and entreat and pursue each other by turns. Suddenly the music stops, and each dancer shows his skill by remaining absolutely motionless, bounding again in the full life of the fandango as the orchestra strikes up. The sound of the guitar, the violin, the rapid tic-tac of heels (*taconeos*), the crack of fingers and castanets, the supple swaying of the dancers, fill the spectators with ecstasy.

" The music whirls along in a rapid triple time. Spangles glitter; the sharp clank of ivory and ebony castanets beats out the cadence of strange, throbbing, deafening notes—assonances unknown to music, but curiously characteristic, effective, and intoxicating. Amidst the rustle of silks, smiles gleam over white teeth, dark eyes sparkle and droop, and flash up again in flame. All is flutter and glitter, grace and animation—quivering, sonorous, passionate, seductive. *Ole! Ole!* Faces beam and burn. *Ole! Ole!*

" The bolero intoxicates, the fandango inflames."

I found the following reference to the fandango in Philip Thicknesse's remarkably interesting and exceedingly curious book, " A Year's Journey through France and Part of Spain " (London : 1777) : " In no part of the world, therefore, are women more caressed and attended to, than in Spain. Their deportment in public is grave and modest; yet they are very much addicted to pleasure; nor is there scarce one among them that cannot, nay, that will not, dance the *Fan-*

dango in private, either in the decent or the indecent manner. I have seen it danced both ways, by a pretty woman, than which nothing can be more *immodestly agreeable* ; and I was shewn a young lady at *Barcelona* who in the midst of this dance ran out of the room, telling her partner she could *stand* it no longer ;—he ran after her, to be sure, and must be answerable for the consequences. I find in the music of the *Fandango*, written under one bar, *Salida*, which signifies *going out* ; it is where the woman is to part a little from her partner, and to move slowly by herself ; and I suppose it was at *that bar the* lady was so overcome, as to determine her not to return.

Philip Thicknesse is one of the undeservedly forgotten figures of the eighteenth century. He wrote twenty-four books, including the first Life of Thomas Gainsborough, whom he claims to have discovered and which contains accounts of pictures which have disappeared, " A Treatise on the Art of Decyphering and of Writing in Cypher with an Harmonic Alphabet," and the aforementioned account of a journey through France and Spain which contains one of the earliest sympathetic descriptions of Montserrat. Thicknesse led far from a dull life and its course was marked by a series of violent quarrels. Born in 1719 he was in Georgia with General Oglethorpe in 1735.

Later he fought wild negroes in Jamaica and cruised in the Mediterranean with Admiral Medley. In 1762 he had a dispute with Francis Vernon (afterwards Lord Orwell and Earl of Shipbrooke) then Colonel of the Suffolk militia ; and having sent the Colonel the ridiculous present of a wooden gun became involved in an action for libel with the result that he was confined three months in the King's Bench Prison and fined £300. He was married three times. For his son, by his second marriage, Baron Audley, he conceived a deep hatred of which there is an echo in his will wherein he desires his right hand to be cut off and sent to Lord Audley to remind him of his duty to God after having so long abandoned the duty he owed to his father. The title of his last book also bears witness to this feud : " Memoirs and Anecdotes of Philip Thicknesse, late Lieutenant Governor of Land Guard Fort and unfortunately father to George Touchet, Baron Audley." In 1774 his twenty year friendship with Gainsborough ended in a wretched squabble. In 1775 a decree of chancery ratified by the House of Lords, to which he appealed, deprived him of what he considered his right to £12,000 from the family of his first wife. Feeling himself driven out of his country, accompanied by his third wife, two children and a monkey, he went to live in Spain, but he was back in England in a year and published the book from which I have quoted. His third wife, Anne Ford, was celebrated as a musician and you may find some account of her in the old Grove's Dictionary. She played the guitar, the viola de gamba, and the "musical glasses" and sang airs by Handel and the early Italians. The customs inspector at Cette on the way to Spain found "a bass viol, two guittars, a fiddle, and some other musical instruments" in Thicknesse's baggage. Thicknesse died in 1792 and was buried in the Protestant Cemetery in Boulogne. The greater part of his work in Spain is devoted to an account of Montserrat, which he visited before its despoliation.

It can be well understood that the study of Spanish dancing and its music must be carried on in Spain. Mr. Ellis tells us why : " Another characteristic of Spanish dancing, and especially of the most typical kind called flamenco, lies in its accompaniments, and particularly in the fact that under proper conditions all the spectators are themselves performers. . . . Thus it is that at the end of a dance an absolute silence often falls, with no sound of applause : the relation of performers and public has ceased to exist. . . . The finest Spanish dancing is at once killed or degraded by the presence of an indifferent or unsympathetic public, and that is probably why it cannot be transplanted, but remains local."

At the end of a dance an absolute silence often falls. . . . I am again in an underground café in Amsterdam. It is the eve of the Queen's birthday, and the Dutch are celebrating. The low, smoke-wreathed room is crowded with students, soldiers, and women. Now a weazened female takes her place at the piano, on a slightly raised platform at one side of the room. She begins to play. The dancing begins. It is not woman with man ; the dancing is informal. Some dance together, and some dance alone ; some sing the melody of the tune, others shriek, but all make a noise. Faster and faster and louder and louder the music is pounded out, and the dancing becomes wilder and wilder. A tray of glasses is kicked from the upturned palm of a sweaty waiter. Waiter, broken glass, dancer, all lie, a laughing heap, on the floor. A soldier and a woman stand in opposite corners, facing the corners ; then without turning, they back towards the middle of the room at a furious pace ; the collision is appalling. Hand in hand the mad dancers encircle the room, throwing confetti, beer, anything. A heavy stein crushes two teeth—the wound bleeds—but the dancer does not stop. Noise and action and colour all become synonymous. There is no escape from the force. I am dragged into the circle. Suddenly the music stops. All the dancers stop. The soldier no longer looks at the woman by his side ; not a word is spoken. People lumber towards chairs. The woman looks for a glass of water to assuage the pain of her bleeding mouth. I think Jaques-Dalcroze is right when he seeks to unite spectator and actor, drama and public,

IV

In the preceding section I may have too strongly insisted upon the relation of the folk-song to the dance. It is true that the two are seldom separated in performance (although not all songs are danced; for example, the *cañas* and *playeras* of Andalusia). However, most of the folk-songs of Spain are intended to be danced; they are built on dance-rhythms and they bear the names of dances. Thus the jota is always danced to the same music, although the variations are great at different times and in different provinces. It is, of course, when the folk-songs are danced that they make their best effect, in the polyrhythm achieved by the opposing rhythms of guitar-player, dancer, and singer. When there is no dancer the defect is sometimes overcome by some one tapping a stick on the ground in imitation of resounding heels.

Blind beggars have a habit of singing the songs, in certain provinces, with a wealth of florid ornament, such ornament as is always associated with oriental airs in performance, and this ornament still plays a considerable rôle when the vocalist becomes an integral part of the accompaniment for a dancer. Chabrier gives several examples of it in one of his letters. In the circumstances it can readily be seen that Spanish folk-songs written down are pretty bare recollections of the real thing, and when sung by singers who have no knowledge of the traditional manner of performing them they are likely to sound fairly banal. The same thing might be said of the negro folk-songs of America, or the folk-songs of Russia or Hungary, but with much less truth, for the folk-songs of these countries usually possess a melodic interest which is seldom inherent in the folk-songs of Spain. To make their effect they must be performed by Spaniards, as nearly as possible after the manner of the people. Indeed, their spirit and their polyrhythmic effects are much more essential to their proper interpretation than their melody, as many witnesses have pointed out.

Spanish music, indeed, much of it, is actually unpleasant to Western ears; it lacks the sad monotony and the wailing intensity of true oriental music; much of it is loud and blaring, like the hot sunglare of the Iberian peninsula. However, many a Western or Northern European has found pleasure in listening by the hour to the strains, which often sound as if they were improvised, sung by some beggar or mountaineer.

The collections of these songs are not in any sense complete and few of them attempt more than a collocation of the songs of one locality or people. Deductions have been drawn. For example it is noted that the Basque songs are irregular in melody and rhythm and are further marked by unusual tempos, 5-8, or 7-4. In Aragon and Navarre the popular song (and dance) is the jota ; in Galicia, the seguidilla ; the Catalonian songs resemble the folk-tunes of Southern France. The Andalusian songs, like the dances of that province, are the most beautiful of all, often truly oriental in their rhythm and floridity. In Spain the gipsy has become an integral part of the popular life, and it is difficult at times to determine what is *flamenco* and what is Spanish. However, collections (few to be sure) have been attempted of gipsy songs.

Elsewhere in this rambling article I have touched on the *villancicos* and the early songwriters. To do justice to these subjects would require a good deal more space and a different intention. Those who are interested in them may pursue these matters in Pedrell's various works. The most available collection of Spanish folktunes is that issued by P. Lacome and J. Puig y Alsubide (Paris, 1872). There are several collections of Basque songs ; Demófilo's " Colección de Cantos Flamencos " (Seville, 1881), Cecilio Ocón's collection of Andalusian folk-songs, and F. Rodríguez Marín's " Cantos Populares Españoles " (Seville, 1882-3) may also be mentioned.

The Spanish catalogue of the Victor Phonograph Company offers a splendid opportunity for the study of Spanish and gipsy folk-music. You may find therein even examples of gipsy songs, conceived in esoteric scales, sung by gipsies, accompanied by the guitar. Mr. Caro-Delvaille has brought to my attention Nos. 62365 (Peteneras) and 62289 (Soleares). Nos. 62078 (Sevillanas and Farrucas) and 62077 (Jotas Nuevas), sung by Pozo, are also good. Most of Pozo's records will be found to be interesting.

When Dimitry Slaviansky visited Barcelona with his Russian choir in 1895, introducing Russian folk-music to Spain, he became very much interested in the folk-music of Cataluña. His enthusiasm was contagious and Spanish musicians themselves caught the fever. In that very year Enrique Morera made a harmonization of the first verse of *Sant Ramon*, a traditional melody from the island of Mallorca, which was performed by the Russian Choir. Later Amadeo Vives founded the Orfeó Catalá, a choral society which devotes itself for the most part to the exploitation of the old folk and religious music, arranged by Morera, Pedrell, and other Spanish composers. Lluis Millet is now the director of this organization, which visited Paris and London in the spring of 1914. In both these cities the Choir was received with enthusiasm. Henry Quittard wrote in " Le Figaro " : " We must confess that we have never heard anything that could approach this extraordinary ensemble." Emile Vuillermoz said, " A most varied program showed all the resources of this miraculous instrument, which ravishes and at the same time humiliates us profoundly. The comparison of our most reputed French choruses with this splendid phalanx is singularly sad for our own pride. Never have we had such discipline in a group which unites voices of such quality. Now we know what can be done. It is impossible to imagine the degree of technical perfection, of collective virtuosity, which human voices can attain, before one has heard the colossal living organ which Lluis Millet has presented Barcelona." Lluis Millet has issued a book with musical illustrations on " The Religious Folk-Song of Spain." On January 15, 1918, the Schola Cantorum of New York under the direction of Kurt Schindler gave a concert at Carnegie Hall in which the major part of the program was devoted to songs in the répertoire of the Orfeó Catalá, sung in the original tongues. Strictly speaking these can no longer be called folk-songs as they have all been rearranged. In some instances, aside from an occasional use of a folk-melody, they may be considered original compositions. Several of the songs were arranged, in some instances one might almost say composed, by Kurt Schindler and presented for the first time in their new form. One of these, *A Miracle of the Virgin Mary*, a fourteenth century canticle of Spanish Galicia, in which Mabel Garrison's lovely voice was assigned an important rôle, proved to be very beautiful. The whole program, indeed, aroused the deepest interest.

V

After the bullfight* the most popular form of amusement in Spain is the zarzuela, the only distinctive art-form which Spanish music has evolved, but there has been no progress ; the form has not changed, except perhaps to degenerate, since its invention in the early seventeeth century. Soriano Fuertes and other writers have devoted pages to grieving because Spanish composers have not taken occasion to make something grander and more important out of the zarzuela. The fact remains that they have not, although, small and great alike, they have all taken a hand at writing these entertainments. But as they found the zarzuela, so they have left it. It must

---

*E. E. Hale (" Seven Spanish Cities ") achieved the almost impossible feat of writing a book about Spain without having seen a bull-fight. One might as well attempt to write a history of opera, after refusing to listen to Wagner's *Ring*. H. T. Finck (" Spain and Morocco ") was satisfied and disgusted with half a bull-fight. His attitude is quoted and reflected in Baedeker. . . . More sympathetic and detailed accounts of this very popular Spanish diversion may be found in Richard Ford's " Gatherings from Spain," Gautier's " Voyage en Espagne," Havelock Ellis's " The Soul of Spain," and de Amicis's " Spain and the Spaniards." Edward Penfield has illustrated a bull-fight in his " Spanish Sketches." The chapter on the bull-fight in John Hay's " Castilian Days " is very readable. Good descriptions of the tauromachian sport may be found in Frank Harris's very vivid story " Montes the Matador " (Gautier, by the way, devotes many nervous pages to Montes) and in Edgar Saltus's early novel, " Mr. Incoul's Misadventure." But the epic of the bull-fight is undoubtedly Blasco Ibañez's *Sangre y Arena* (translated as *Blood and Sand*).

be conceded that the form is quite distinct from that of opera and should not be confused with it. And the Spaniards are probably right when they assert that the zarzuela is the mother of the French opéra-bouffe. At least it must be admitted that Offenbach and Lecocq and their precursors owe something of the germ of their inspiration to the Spanish form. To-day the melody chests of the zarzuela markets are plundered to find tunes for French *revues*, and such popular airs as *La Paraguaya* and *Y . . . Como le Vá?* were originally danced and sung in Spanish theatres. The composer of these airs, J. Valverde *fils*, indeed found the French market so good that he migrated to Paris, and for some time wrote *musique mélangée . . . une moitié de chaque nation*. So *La Rose de Grenade*, composed for Paris, might have been written for Spain, with slight melodic alterations and tauromachian allusions in the book.

The zarzuela is usually a one-act piece (although sometimes it is permitted to run into two or more acts) in which the music is freely interrupted by spoken dialogue, and that in turn gives way to national dances. Very often the entire score is danced as well as sung. The subject is usually comic and often topical, although it may be serious, poetic, or even tragic. The actors often introduce dialogue of their own,* " gagging "

---

*This is no longer true, Mr. John Garrett Underhill informs me, as the Sociedad de Autores has forbidden such interpolations.

freely; sometimes they engage in long impromptu conversations with members of the audience. They also embroider on the music after the fashion of the great singers of the old Italian opera (Cart de Lafontaine asserts that Spanish audiences, even in cabarets, demand embroidery of this sort). The music is spirited and lively, and in the dances, Andalusian, *flamenco*, or Sevillan, as the case may be, it attains its best results. H. V. Hamilton, in his essay on the subject in Grove's Dictionary, says, " The music is . . . apt to be vague in form when the national dance and folk-song forms are avoided. The orchestration is a little blatant." It will be seen that this description suits Granados's *Goyescas* (the opera), which is on its safest ground during the dances and becomes excissively vague at other times; but *Goyescas* is not a zarzuela, because there is no spoken dialogue. Otherwise it bears the earmarks. A zarzuela stands somewhere between a French *revue* and opéra-comique. It is usually, however, more informal in tone than the latter and often decidedly more serious than the former. All the musicians in Spain since the form was invented (excepting, of course, certain exclusively religious composers), and most of the poets and playwrights, have contributed numerous examples. Thus Calderon wrote the first zarzuela, and Lope de Vega contributed words to entertainments much in the same order. In our day Miguel Echegaray, brother of José Echegaray, has written one of the most popular zarzuelas, *Gigantes y Cabezudos* (the music by Caballero). The subject is the fiesta of Santa Maria del Pilar It has had many a long run and is often revived. Another very popular zarzuela is *La Gran Via* (by Valverde, *père*), which has been performed in London in extended form. The principal theatres for the zarzuela in Madrid are (or were until recently) that of the Calle de Jovellanos, called the Teatro de Zarzuela, and the Apolo. Usually four separate zarzuelas are performed in one evening before as many audiences.

At the Apolo, " the evening is divided into separate sections—four or five are the usual number," writes Mr. John Garrett Underhill. " These are called *funciones*, each consisting of a single play. If the first *función* begins at eight, the second will follow at nine or nine-fifteen, the third at ten, the fourth shortly after eleven, and the last, which is commonly a farce, appealing perhaps to the less puritanical elements in the community, at twelve or a quarter after twelve. A similar system prevails in the afternoons. There is considerable variation in the hours of the *funciones* in different cities, according to the character and habits of the population. In some theatres performances are practically continuous. . . . A separate admission is charged to each *función*. . . . Spacious and comfortable waiting rooms are provided in which the audience gathers for the succeeding *función* previously to the conclusion of that actually in progress, so that the delay incident to the necessary change is reduced to a minimum, never exceeding a quarter of an hour. Meanwhile ushers circulate through the aisles and boxes taking up the tickets of those who remain, although in these popular theatres the reconstitution of the audience is practically complete."

Mr. Underhill further says, anent the zarzuela: " The zarzuela was originally a three act romantic operetta, partly sung and partly spoken, and it continued in this form until the introduction of the one act form in the early eighties. The performances given at the Teatro de Zarzuela were mostly in the more elaborate form, while the *género chico* (lesser genre) made its home at the Apolo. With the change to one act, the zarzuelas became more realistic—minute pictures of local customs, etc., built up around characteristic songs and dances, so that now the name has come to be pretty well synonymous with this species of entertainment, while the longer older form is generally spoken of as operetta. In other words a zarzuela is rather a musico-dramatic entertainment that is strongly Spanish than merely a mixed form. *The Land of Joy* illustrates precisely this quality, although, having no dramatic element, it is not a zarzuela.

" The most popular zarzuelas are all strongly coloured. They are *La Alegría de la Huerta*, music by Federico Chueca, built up about a scene of provincial merry-making, *La Verbena de la Paloma* by Bretón, dealing with a popular religious festival in Madrid, Manuel Nieto's *Certamen Nacional*, Fernàndez Caballero's *El Cabo Primero* and *Gigantes y Cabezudos*, and Chapi's *El Puñao de Rosas*. All these are in one act and the spoken parts are broad low comedy. To these must be added Emilio Arrieta's *Marina*, in three acts, the best example of the old form, showing strong Italian influence. *Marina* is the sort of operatic classic with Spaniards that *Pinafore*—another nautical work—is with us.

"What is most distinctive in the zarzuela is its low comedy and Spanish *sal*, together with that peculiar indiscipline so well exemplified by *The Land of Joy*. In other words, the zarzuela is a state of mind, just as Spanish music is an expression of Spanish life, and unintelligible without some understanding of its symbols.

"It would be safe to say that every zarzuela has either a realistic low comedy element or otherwise exhibits some direct form of theatricalism, differentiating it in this respect from works of a purely artistic category. Yet it is difficult to draw the line. The zarzuela is not without a tang similar to that of our burlesque stage. The analogue would be American burlesque written by playwrights of high intelligence. Had Harrigan's *Mulligan Guards Ball* been compressed into one act, it would have been a typical zarzuela."

La Gran Via, which in some respects may be considered a typical zarzuela, consists of a string of dance-tunes, with no more homogeneity than their national significance would suggest. There is an introduction and polka, a waltz, a tango, a jota, a mazurka, a schottische, another waltz, and a two-step (*paso-doble*). The tunes have little distinction; nor can the orchestration be considered brilliant. There is a great deal of noise and variety of rhythm, and when presented correctly the effect must be precisely that of one of the dance-halls described by Chabrier. The zarzuela, to be fully enjoyed, in fact, must be seen in Spain. Like Spanish dancing it requires a special audience to bring out its best points. There must be a certain electricity, at least an element of sympathy, to carry the thing through successfully. Examination of the scores of zarzuelas (many of them have been printed and some of them are to be seen in our libraries) will convince any one that Mr. Ellis is speaking mildly when he says that the Spaniards love noise. However, the combination of this noise with beautiful women, dancing, elaborate rhythm, and a shouting audience, seems to almost equal the café-concert dancing and the tauromachian spectacles in Spanish popular affection. (Of course, as I have suggested, there are zarzuelas more serious melodically and dramatically; but as *La Gran Via* is frequently mentioned by writers as one of the most popular examples, it may be selected as typical of the larger number of these entertainments.)

H. V. Hamilton says that the first performance of a zarzuela took place in 1628 (Pedrell gives the date as October 29, 1629), during the reign of Felipe IV, in the Palace of the Zarzuela (so called because it was surrounded by *zarzas*, brambles). It was called *El Jardín de Falerina*; the text was by the great Calderon and the music by Juan Risco, chapelmaster of the cathedral at Cordova, according to Mr. Hamilton, who doubtless follows Soriano Fuertes on this detail. Soubies, following the more modern studies of Pedrell, gives José Peyró the credit. Pedrell, in his richly documented work, " Teatro Lírico Español anterior al siglo XIX," attributes the music of this zarzuela to Peyró and gives an example of it. The first Spanish opera dates from the same period, Lope de Vega's *La Selva sin Amor* (1629). As a matter of fact, many of the plays of Calderon and Lope de Vega were performed with music to heighten the effect of the declamation, and musical curtain-raisers and interludes were performed before and in the midst of all of them. Lana, Palomares, Benavente and Hidalgo were among the musicians who contributed music to the theatre of this period. Hidalgo wrote the music for Calderon's zarzuela, *Ni Amor se Libra de Amor*. To the same group belong Miguel Ferrer, Juan de Navas, Sebastian Durón, and Jerónimo de la Torre. (Examples of the music of these men may be found in the aforementioned "Teatro Lírico.") Until 1659 zarzuelas were written by the best poets and composers and frequently performed on royal birthdays, at royal marriages, and on many other occasions; but after that date the art fell into a decline and seems to have been in eclipse during the whole of the eighteenth century. According to Soriano Fuertes the beginning of the reign of Felipe V marked the introduction of Italian opera into Spain (more popular than Spanish opera there to this day) and the decadence of nationalism (whole pages of Fuertes read very much like the plaints of modern English composers about the neglect of national composers in their country). In 1829 there was a revival of interest in Spanish music and a conservatory was founded in Madrid. (For a discussion of this later period the reader is referred to "La Opera Española en el Siglo XIX," by Antonio Peña y Goñi, 1881.) This interest has been fostered by Fuertes and Pedrell, and the younger composers to-day are taking some account of it. There is hope, indeed, that Spanish music may again take its place in the world of art.

Of course, the zarzuela did not spring into being out of nowhere and nothing, and the true origins are not entirely obscure. It is generally agreed that a priest, Juan del Enzina (born at Salamanca, 1468), was the true founder of the secular theatre in Spain. His dramatic compositions are in the nature of eclogues based on Virgilian models. In all of these there is singing and in one a dance. Isabel la Católica in the fifteenth century always had at her command a troop of musicians and poets who comforted and consoled her in her chapel with motets and *plegarias* (French, *prière*), and in the royal apartments with *canciones* and *villancicos*. (*Canciones* are songs inclining towards the ballad-form. *Villancicos* are songs in the old Spanish measure ; they receive their name from their rustic character, as supposedly they were first composed by the *villanos* or peasants for the nativity and other festivals of the church.) (On the program of the second historical concert given by M. Fétis in Paris, November 18, 1832, devoted to music of the sixteenth century, I find : " *Villancicos espagnols, a 6 voix de femmes, avec 8 guitars obligées, composés par Soto de Puebla et exécutés dans un concert a la cour de Philippe II* [1561].") " It is necessary to search for the true origins of the Spanish musical spectacle," states Soubies, " in the *villancicos* and *cantarcillos* which alternated with the dialogue in the works of Juan del Enzina and Lucas Fernández, without forgetting the *ensaladas*, the *jácaras*, etc., which served as intermezzi and curtain-raisers." These were sung before the curtain, before the drama was performed (and during the intervals, with jokes added) by women in court dress, and later created a form of their own (besides contributing to the creation of the zarzuela), the *tonadilla*, which, accompanied by a guitar or violin and interspersed with dances, was very popular for a number of years. H. V. Hamilton is probably on sound ground when he says, " That the first zarzuela was written with an express desire for expansion and development is, however, not so certain as that it was the result of a wish to inaugurate the new house of entertainment with something entirely original and novel."*

---

*George Henry Lewes gives some account of the drama in Spain, touching on the zarzuela, in Chapter XIV of " On Actors and the Art of Acting."

VI

We have Richard Ford's testimony that Spain was not very musical in his day. Mr. Henry Cart de Lafontaine says that the contemporary musical services in the churches are not to be considered seriously from an artistic point of view. Emmanuel Chabrier was impressed with the fact that the music for dancing was almost entirely rhythmic in its effect, strummed rudely on the guitar, the spectators meanwhile making such a din that it was practically impossible to distinguish a melody, had there been one. And all observers point at the Italian opera, which is still the favourite opera in Spain (in Barcelona at the Liceo three weeks of opera in Catalan is given after the regular season in Italian; in Madrid at the Teatro-Real the Spanish season is scattered through the Italian), and at Señor Arbós's concerts (the same Señor Arbós who was once concert master of the Boston Symphony Orchestra), at which Brandenburg concertos and Beethoven symphonies are more frequently performed than works by Albéniz.* Still there are, and have

---

*In Gautier's day Bellini was the favourite composer (see P. 215, "Voyage en Espagne").

John Hay writes in "Castilian Days" (1871): "It (Madrid) has a superb opera house, which might as well be in Naples, for all the national character it has; the Court Theatre, where not a word of Castilian is ever heard, nor a strain of Spanish music . . . . The champagny

always been during the course of the last century, Spanish composers, some of whom have made a little noise in the outer world, although a good many have been content to spend their artistic energy on the manufacture of zarzuelas—in other words, to make a good deal of noise in Spain. In most modern instances, however, there has been a revival of interest in the national forms, and folk-song and folk-dance have contributed their important share to the composers' work. No one man has done more to encourage this interest in nationalism than Felipe Pedrell, who may be said to have begun in Spain the work which " the Five " accomplished in Russia. Pedrell says in his " Handbook " (Barcelona, 1891 ; Heinrich and Co. ; French translation by Bertal ; Paris, Fischbacher) : " The popular song, the voice of the people, the pure primitive inspiration of the anonymous singer, passes through the alembic of contemporary art and one obtains thereby its quintessence ; the composer assimilates it and then reveals it in the most delicate form that music alone is capable of, rendering form in its

strains of Offenbach are heard in every town of Spain oftener than the ballads of the country. In Madrid there are more *pilluelos* who whistle *Bu qui s'avance* than the Hymn of Riego. The Cancan has taken its place on the boards of every stage in the city, apparently to stay ; and the exquisite jota and cachucha are giving way to the bestialities of the Casino Cadet."

It is well to remember in this connection that the Metropolitan Opera House in New York and Covent Garden Theatre in London " might as well be in Naples " too, " for all the national character " they have. Our symphony orchestras, too, perform works by native composers as infrequently as those in Madrid.

technical aspect, thanks to the extraordinary development of the technique of our art in this epoch. The folk-song lends the accent, the background, and modern art lends all that it possesses, its conventional symbolism and the richness of form which is its patrimony. The frame is enlarged in such a fashion that the *lied* makes a corresponding development ; could it be said then that the national lyric drama is the same *lied* expanded ? Is not the national lyric drama the product of the force of absorption and creative power ? Do we not see in it faithfully reflected not only the artistic idiosyncrasy of each composer, but all the artistic manifestations of the people ? " There is always the search for new composers in Spain and always the hope that a man may come who will be acclaimed by the world. As a consequence, the younger composers in Spain often receive more adulation than is their due. It must be remembered that the most successful Spanish music is not serious; the Spanish are more themselves in the lighter vein.

I hesitate for a moment on the name of Martin y Soler, born at Valencia ; died at St. Petersburg, 1806 ; called " The Italian " by the Spaniards on account of his musical style, and " lo Spagnuolo " by the Italians. Da Ponte wrote several opera-books for him, *l'Arbore di Diana, la Cosa Rara,* and *La Capricciosa Coretta* (a version of *The Taming of the Shrew*) among others. It is to be seen that he is without importance if considered as a composer distinctively Spanish, and I have made this slight reference to him solely to recount how Mozart quoted an air from one of his operas in the supper scene of *Don Giovanni*. At the time, Martin y Soler was better liked in Vienna than Mozart himself, and the air in question was as well known as say Musetta's waltz is known to us.

Juan Chrysostomo Arriaga, born in Bilbao 1808 ; died 1828 (these dates are given in Grove : 1806-1826), is another matter. He might have become better known had he lived longer. As it is, some of his music has been performed in London and Paris, and perhaps in America, although I have no record of it. He studied in Paris at the Conservatoire, under Fétis for harmony, and Baillot for violin. Before he went to Paris even, as a child, with no knowledge of the rules of harmony, he had written an opera ! Cherubini declared his fugue for eight voices on the words in the Credo, " Et Vitam Venturi," a veritable chef d'œuvre, at least there is a legend to this effect. In 1824 he wrote three quartets, an overture, a symphony, a mass, and some French cantatas and romances. Garcia considered his opera *Los Esclavos Felices* so good that he attempted, unsuccessfully, to secure for it a Paris hearing. It has been performed in Bilbao, which city, I think, celebrated the centenary of the composer's birth.

Manuel Garcia is better known to us as a singer, an impresario, and a father, than as a composer ! Still he wrote a good deal of music (so did Mme. Malibran ; for a list of the diva's compositions I must refer the reader to Arthur Pougin's biography). Fétis enumerates seventeen Spanish, nineteen Italian, and seven French operas by Garcia. He had works produced in Madrid, at the Opéra in Paris (*La mort du Tasse* and *Florestan*), at the Italiens in Paris (*Fazzoletto*), at the Opéra-Comique in Paris (*Deux Contrats*), and at many other theatres. However, when all is said and done, Manuel Garcia's reputation still rests on his singing and his daughters. His compositions are forgotten ; nor was his music, much of it probably, truly Spanish. (However, I have heard a polo [serenade] from an opera called *El Poeta Calculista*, which is so Spanish in accent and harmony—and so beautiful—that it has found a place in a collection of folk-tunes !)

Miguel Hilarión Eslava (born in Burlada, October 21, 1807, died at Madrid, July 23, 1878) is chiefly famous for his compilation, the " Lira Sacra-Hispana," mentioned heretofore. He also composed over 140 pieces of church music, masses, motets, songs, etc., after he had been appointed chapelmaster of Queen Isabella in 1844, and several operas, including *El Solitario, La Tregua del Ptolemaide*, and *Pedro el Cruél*. He also wrote several books of theory and composition : " Método de Solfeo " (1846) and " Escuela de Armonía y Composición " in three parts (harmony, composition, and melody). He edited (1855-6) the " Gaceta Musical de Madrid."

There is the celebrated virtuoso, Pablo de Sarasate, who wrote music, but his memory is perhaps better preserved in Whistler's diabolical portrait than in his own compositions.

To fill in the period between 1850-70 four names are necessary, those of Joaquín Gatzambide, Emilio Arrieta, Baltasar Saldoni, and Francisco A. Barbieri. Joaquín Gatzambide, born February 7, 1822, was a pupil of the Madrid Conservatory, and conductor of the " Pensions " concerts at the Conservatory. He was the composer of at least forty zarzuelas of which some of the titles follow : *La Cisterna Encantada*, *La Edad en la Boca*, *Matilda y Malek Adel*, *El Secreto de la Reina*, *Las Señas del Archiduque*, and *El Valle de Andorra*. He died March 18, 1870.

Emilio Arrieta, born October 21, 1823, was a pupil of the Milan Conservatory from 1842 until 1845. Many of the best Spanish musicians have received their training outside of Spain. His first opera, *Ildegonda*, was produced at Milan. He returned to Spain in 1848. In 1857 he became a teacher of composition in the Madrid Conservatory and later became director of that institution. He died February 11, 1894. The extensive list of his zarzuelas and operas (there are about fifty altogether) includes the following titles : *La Conquista de Granada*, *La Dama del Rey*, *De Madrid á Biarritz*, *Los Enemigos Domes-*

ticos, La Tabernera de Londres, Un Viaje á Cochinchina, and *La Vuelta del Corsario*. His most popular work is *Marina*.

Francisco Asenjo Barbieri, born at Madrid, August 3, 1823, studied in the Conservatory there and after a varied career as member of a military band, a theatre orchestra, and an Italian opera troupe, became secretary and chief promoter of an association for instituting a Spanish national opera and encouraging the production of zarzuelas, in opposition to the Italian opera. *Gloria y Peluca* (1850), *Jugar con Fuego* (1851) were the first of these zarzuelas, of which he wrote seventy-five in all. He was also a teacher and a critic. He died in Madrid, February 19, 1894.

Baltasar Saldoni (1807-1890), born at Barcelona and educated at the monastery of Montserrat, was organist and teacher as well as composer. His works include a symphony for orchestra, military band and organ, *A mi patria*, a *Hymn to the God of Art*, operas and zarzuelas, and a great quantity of church and organ music.

Felipe Pedrell (born February 19, 1841) is also perhaps more important as a writer on musical subjects and for his influence on the younger school of composers (he teaches in the conservatory of Barcelona, and his attitude towards nationalism has already been discussed), than he is as a composer. Still, Edouard Lopez-Chavarri does not hesitate to pronounce his trilogy *Los Pireneos* (Barcelona, 1902 ; the prologue was performed in Venice in 1897) the most important work for the theatre written in Spain. His first opera, *El Ultimo Abencerraje*, was produced in Barcelona in 1874. Some of his other works are *Quasimodo*, 1875 ; *El Tasso á Ferrara*, *Cleopatra*, *Mazeppa* (Madrid, 1881), *La Celestina* (1904), and *La Matinada* (1905). *El Ultimo Abencerraje* was sung in Italian when it was produced in Barcelona in 1874. *Quasimodo* is an operatic version of Victor Hugo's " Notre-Dame de Paris." *Mazeppa* (after Byron) is in one act as is *Tasso* ; *Cleopatra* is in four acts. *Los Pirenos* is the first part of a triptych of which *La Celestina* is the second. The three parts are named respectively, Fatherland, Love, and Faith. So far as I know the third part has not yet appeared. *La Matinada* is called " a musical landscape," for solo, chorus, and an invisible orchestra.

Henri de Curzon, who translated *La Celestina* into French, has an exhaustive and extremely interesting account of Pedrell in " La Nouvelle Revue," Vol. 25, P. 72, under the title " Un maître de la Musique Espagnole." A highly laudatory essay on *La Celestina* by Camille Bellaigue may be found in his book entitled, " Notes Brèves." Bellaigue tells how he received the score in 1903 but only found time to study it during the rainy summer of 1910. His enthusiasm is unrestrained although he has not heard the work performed. The title of the essay is

"Un Tristan Espagnol" and he says: "la joie et la douleur, l'amour et la mort partout se touchent et se fondent ici. De leur contact et de leur fusion, jamais encore une fois, depuis *Tristan*, l'art lyrique n'avait aussi fortement exprime le sombre mystère." He calls the work "le plus originale et le plus admirable peut-être, après *Boris Godunoff*, qui, depuis les temps déjà lointains de *Falstaff*, nous soit venu de l'étranger." J. A. Fuller-Maitland says that the influence of Wagner is traceable in all Pedrell's stage work. (Wagner was adored in Spain; *Parsifal* was given eighteen times in one month at the Liceo in Barcelona.) If this be true, his case will be found to bear other resemblances to that of the Russian "Five," who found it difficult to exorcise all foreign influences in their pursuit of nationalism.

He was made a member of the Spanish Academy in 1894 and shortly thereafter became Professor of Musical History and Æsthetics at the Royal Conservatory at Madrid. Besides his "Hispaniae Schola Musica Sacra" he has written a number of other books, and translated Richter's treatise on Harmony into Spanish. He has made several excursions into the history of folk-lore and the principal results are contained in " Músicos Anónimos " and " Por nuestra Música." Other works are " Teatro Lírico Español anterior al siglo XIX," " Lírica Nacionalizada," " De Música Religiosa," " Músiquerias y mas Músiquerias." One of his books, "Músicos Contemporáneos y de Otros Tiempos" is very catholic in its range of subject. It includes essays on the *Don Quixote* of Strauss, the *Boris Godunoff* of Musorgsky, Smetana, Manuel Garcia, Edward Elgar, Jaques-Dalcroze, Bruckner, Mahler, Albéniz, Palestrina, Busoni, and the tenth symphony of Beethoven!

In John Towers's extraordinary compilation, "Dictionary-Catalogue of Operas," it is stated that Manuel Fernández Caballero (born in 1835) wrote sixty-two operas, and the names of them are given. He was a pupil of Fuertes (harmony) and Eslava (composition) at the Madrid Conservatory and later became very popular as a writer of zarzuelas. I have already mentioned his *Gigantes y Cabezudos* for which Miguel Echegaray furnished the book. Among his other works in this form are *Los Dineros del Sacristán*, *Los Africanistas* (Barcelona, 1894), *El Cabo Primero* (Barcelona, 1895), and *La Rueda de la Fortuna* (Madrid, 1896).

At a concert given in the New York Hippodrome, April 3, 1911, Mme. Tetrazzini sang a Spanish song, which was referred to the next day by the reviewers of the "New York Times" and the "New York Globe." To say truth the soprano made a great effect with the song, although it was written for a low voice. It was *Carceleras*, from Ruperto Chapí's zarzuela *Las Hijas de Zebedeo*. Chapí was one of the most prolific and popular composers of Spain during the last century. He produced countless zarzuelas and nine children. He was born at Villena, March 27, 1851, and he died March 25, 1909, a few months earlier than his compatriot Isaac Albéniz. He was admitted to the conservatory of Madrid in 1867 as a pupil of piano and harmony. In 1869 he obtained the first prize for harmony and he continued to obtain prizes until in 1874 he was sent to Rome by the Academy of Fine Arts. He remained for some time in Italy and Paris. In 1875 the Teatro Real of Madrid played his *La Hija de Jefté* sent from Rome. The following is an incomplete list of his operas and zarzuelas : *Via Libre*, *Los Gendarmes*, *El Rey que Rabió* (3 acts), *El Cura del Regimiento*, *El Reclamo*, *La Tempestad*, *La Bruja*, *La Leyenda del Monje*, *Las Campanadas*, *La Czarina*, *El Milagro de la Virgen*, *Roger de Flor* (3 acts), *Las Naves de Cortés*, *Circe* (3 acts), *Aqui Hase Farta un Hombre*, *Juan Francisco* (3 acts, 1905 ; rewritten and presented in 1908 as *Entre Rocas*), *Los Madrileños* (1908), *La Dama Roja* (1 act, 1908), *Hesperia* (1908), *Las Calderas de Pedro Botero* (1909) and *Margarita la Tornera*, presented just before his death without success.

Manrique de Lara says of *La Bruja :* " This score of our greatest composer broke abruptly with the Italian tradition which, in form at least, had enslaved our musical productions until that time. A new influence, having its high origin in works of pure classical style whether symphonic or dramatic, led our steps down fresh pathways in *La Bruja*."

His other works include an oratorio, *Los Angeles*, a symphonic poem, *Escenas de Capa y Espada*, a symphony in D, *Moorish Fantasy* for orchestra, a serenade for orchestra, a trio for piano, violin and 'cello, songs, etc. Chapí was president of the Society of Authors and Composers, and when he died the King and Queen of Spain sent a telegram of condolence to his widow. There is a copy of his zarzuela, *Blasones y Talegas* in the New York Public Library.

I have already spoken of *La Dolores*. It is one of a long series of operas and zarzuelas written by Tomás Bretón y Hernandez (born at Salamanca, December 29, 1850). First produced at Madrid, in 1895, it has been sung with success in such distant capitals as Buenos Ayres and Prague. I have been assured by a Spanish woman of impeccable taste that *La Dolores* is charming, delightful in its fluent melody and its striking rhythms, thoroughly Spanish in style, but certain to find favour in America, if it were produced here. Our own Eleanora de Cisneros at a Press Club Benefit in Barcelona appeared in Bretón's zarzuela *La Verbena de la Paloma*. Saint-Saëns admires this work so much that he committed it to memory and plays and replays it on his piano. Another of Bretón's famous zarzuelas is *Los Amantes de Teruel* (Madrid), 1889). His works for the theatre further include *Tabaré*, for which he wrote both words and music (Madrid, 1913) ; *Don Gil* (Barcelona, 1914) ; *Garín* (Barcelona, 1891) ; *Raquel* (Madrid, 1900) ; *Guzmán el Bueno* (Madrid, 1876) ; *El Certamen de Cremona* (Madrid, 1906) ; *El Campanero de Begoña* (Madrid, 1878) ; *El Barberillo en Orán* ; *Corona contra Corona* (Madrid, 1879) ; *Los Amores de un Príncipe* (Madrid, 1881) ; *El Clavel Rojo* (1899) ; *Covadonga* (1901) ; and *El Domingo de Ramos*, words by Echegaray (Madrid, 1894). His works for orchestra include : *En la Alhambra*, *Los Galeotes*, and *Escenas Andaluzas*, a suite. He has written three string quartets, a piano trio, a piano quintet, and an oratorio in two parts, *El Apocalipsis*.

Bretón is largely self-taught, and there is a legend that he devoured by himself Eslava's " School of Composition." He further wrote the music and conducted for a circus for a period of years. In the late seventies he conducted an orchestra, founding a new society, the Union Artística Musical, which is said to have been the beginning of the modern movement in Spain. It may throw some light on Spanish musical taste at this period to mention the fact that the performance of Saint-Saëns' *Danse macabre* almost created a riot. Later Bretón travelled. He appeared as conductor in London, Prague, and Buenos Ayres, among other cities outside of Spain, and when Dr. Karl Muck left Prague for Berlin, he was invited to succeed him in the

Bohemian capital. In the contest held by the periodical " Blanco y Negro " in 1913 to decide who was the most popular writer, poet, painter, musician, sculptor, and toreador in Spain, Bretón as musician got the most votes. . . . He is at present the head of the Royal Conservatory in Madrid.

Emilio Serrano was born in the Basque city of Vitoria. He went early to Madrid, where he studied the piano under Zabalza and composition, at the Conservatory, with both Eslava and Arrieta. While very young he began to write zarzuelas, the best of which belonging to this period is probably *El Juicio de Friné.* His opera, *Mithradates*, in the Italian manner, was produced in 1882 at the Teatro Real in Madrid. Later he produced at the same house *Doña Juana la Loca* and *Irene de Otranto*, for which José Echegaray supplied the libretto. He wrote his own book for *Gonzalo de Córdoba,* an opera in a prologue and three acts (1898). His latest opera, *La Maja de Numbo*, designed for the Lírico (now the Gran) has been performed only in Buenos Ayres. He has written a quartet, a symphony, a piano concerto and at least two symphonic poems, *La Primera Salida de Don Quijote* and *Los Molinos de Viento*. Emilio Serrano succeeded Arrieta as professor of composition at the Madrid Conservatory and there are few Spanish composers of the past two decades who have not been his pupils.

No Spanish composer (ancient or modern) is

TOMÁS BRETÓN

better known outside of Spain than Isaac Albéniz (born May 29, 1860, at Comprodon; died at Cambó, in the Pyrenees, May 25, 1909). His fame rests almost entirely on twelve piano pieces (in four books) entitled collectively *Iberia*, with which concert goers are familiar. They have been performed by Ernest Schelling, Arthur Rubinstein, Leo Ornstein, and George Copeland, among other virtuosi. . . . I think one or two of these pieces must be in the répertoire of every modern pianist. Albéniz did not imbibe his musical culture in Spain and to the day of his death he was more friendly with the modern French group of composers than with those of his native land. He studied at Paris with Marmontel; at Brussels with Louis Brassin; and at Weimar with Liszt (he is mentioned in the long list of pupils in Huneker's biography of Liszt, but there is no further account of him in that book); he studied composition with Jadassohn, Joseph Dupont, and F. Kufferath. His symphonic poem, *Catalonia*, has been performed in Paris by the Colonne Orchestra. Sir Henry J. Wood conducted a performance in London, March 4, 1900. I have no record of any American performance. For a time he devoted himself to the piano. He was a virtuoso and he has even played in London, but later in life he gave up this career for composition. He wrote several operas and zarzuelas, among them a light opera, *The Magic Opal* (produced in London, 1893),

Enrico Clifford (Barcelona, 1894; later heard in London), *Pepita Jiménez* (Barcelona, 1896; afterwards given at the Théâtre de la Monnaie in Brussels), and *San Antonio de la Florida* (produced in Brussels as *l'Ermitage Fleurie*). He left unfinished at his death a trilogy on the subject of King Arthur, *Merlin*, *Lancelot*, and *Ginevra*. None of his operas, with the exception of *Pepita Jiménez*, which has been performed, I am told, in all Spanish countries, achieved any particular success, and it is *Iberia* and a few other piano pieces which serve to keep his memory green.

G. Jean-Aubry writes of this composer : " One and all the young composers of Spain owe to him a debt. Albéniz is Spain, as Musorgsky is Russia, Grieg Norway, and Chopin Poland. . . . *Iberia* marks the summit of the art of Albéniz. Albéniz alone could venture to place this title, both simple and proud, at the head of the twelve divisions of this poem. One finds here all that emotion and culture can desire. The composer here reached a sureness of touch and grasped an originality of technique which demand much attention and which have no ulterior object. He even at times sacrificed perfection of form. There are no doubt fastidious critics who will find blemishes, but such blemishes as exist are not detrimental to expression, and this alone is important. In music there are many excellent scholars but few poets. Albéniz has all the power of the poet—ease and richness of style, beauty and originality of imagery, and a rare sense of suggestion. . . . The *Preludes* and *Studies* of Chopin, the *Carneval* and *Kreisleriana* of Schumann, the *Years of Pilgrimage* of Liszt, the *Prelude, Choral and Fugue*, and the *Prelude, Aria and Finale* of Franck, the *Islamey* of Balakireff, the *Estampes* and *Images* of Debussy, and the twelve poems of *Iberia* will mark the supreme heights of music for the pianoforte since 1830."

Juan Bautista Pujol (1836-1898) gained considerable reputation in Spain as a pianist and as a teacher of and composer for that instrument. He also wrote a method for piano students titled " Nuevo Mecanismo del Piano." His further claim to attention is due to the fact that he was one of the teachers of Granados.

The names of Pahissa (both as conductor and composer ; one of his symphonic works is called *The Combat*), García Robles, represented by an *Epitalame*, and Gibert, with two *Marines*, occur on the programs of the two concerts devoted in the main to Spanish music, at the second of which (Barcelona, 1910 ; conductor Franz Beidler) Granados's *Dante* was performed.

E. Fernández Arbós (born in Madrid, December 25, 1863) is better known as a conductor and violinist than as composer. Still, he has written music, especially for his own instrument. He was a pupil of both Vieuxtemps and Joachim ; and he has travelled much, teaching at the Hamburg

Conservatory, and acting as concertmaster for the Boston Symphony and the Glasgow Orchestras. He has been a professor at the Madrid conservatory for some time, giving orchestral and chamber music concerts, both there and in London. He has written at least one light opera, presumably a zarzuela, *El Centro de la Tierra* (Madrid; December 22, 1895); three trios for piano and strings, songs, and an orchestral suite.

I have already referred to the Valverdes, father and son. The father, in collaboration with Federico Chueca, wrote *La Gran Via*. Many another popular zarzuela is signed by him. The son lived so long in France that much of his music is cast in the style of the French music hall; too it is in a popular vein. Still, in his best tangos he strikes a Spanish folk-note not to be despised. He wrote the music for the play, *La Maison de Danses*, produced, with Polaire, at the Vaudeville in Paris, and two of his operettas, *La Rose de Grenade* and *l'Amour en Espagne*, have been performed in Paris, not without success, I am told by La Argentina, who danced in them. Valverde died in the city of Mexico November 7, 1918.

Tradition and often necessity have driven many Spanish composers out of the peninsula to make their careers abroad. Victoria went to Rome; Arrieta to Milan; Albéniz, Valverde, de Falla (and how many others!) to Paris. Of late, indeed, Paris has been the haven of ambitious Spanish composers who have been received with open arms by their French confrères and where their music has been played by Ricardo Viñes, the Spanish pianist, and by J. Joachim Nin, the Cuban pianist. Viñes, indeed, has been friendly to the moderns of all nations. His programs embrace works of Satie, Albéniz, and Ravel . . . doubtless, indeed, Leo Ornstein.

As a result, some of the zarzuela writers who have stayed at home have produced more characteristic Spanish music than some of their more ambitious brethren. One of the reasons is explained by Mr. Underhill in his essay on the Spanish one-act play: " Spaniards are very particular about these things (the strict Spanish tradition without foreign influence). They insist upon the national element, upon the perpetuation of indigenous forms of expression, both in the matter of literary type and convention, and in mere questions of speech as well. Few writers of the first rank belonging to the past generation have escaped reproach upon this score. They were expected not only to spring from the soil but to taste of it." Equal demands are made upon the zarzuela writers. As a consequence the zarzuela, although scarcely taken seriously by either Spanish musicians or public, and always, according to the pedants, in a tottering decadent stage, may be considered the most national form of Spanish musical art.

I have referred to Joaquín Valverde and his music has become comparatively familiar to

Americans through *The Land of Joy*. José Serrano is another of the popular zarzuela writers. Perhaps his best-known work is *El Mal de Amores* for which the Brothers Quintero furnished the book. Serrano's home is in Madrid where he belongs to Benavente's *tertulia*. In the season of 1916-17 he organized a company for the purpose of presenting his operas and zarzuelas and conducted a campaign in the provinces. He was especially successful in Valencia. His three-act opera, *La Canción del Olvido*, was first performed during this tour. He recently rented the Zarzuela Theatre in Madrid and has continued to give his own and other composers' works there, including Usandizaga's posthumous *La Llama*. Other works of Serrano are *La Reina Mora* (zarzuela in one act, book by the Quinteros) and *La Canción del Soldado*.

Here also I might mention Gerónimo Giménez, who was born in Seville. As a boy he went to Cadiz, studying with his father and singing in the cathedral. At sixteen he conducted a performance of an opera by Petrella at Gibraltar, and in consequence became the conductor of a number of Italian opera companies touring Spain and Portugal. The Province of Cadiz granting him a pension for foreign study, he entered the Paris Conservatory under Ambroise Thomas. He also lived for a time in Milan. Returning to Spain he was engaged by Chapí, who then controlled the Teatro Apolo at Madrid, to direct the orchestra at the production of his new *El Milagro de la Virgen*. Later at the Zarzuela Theatre he conducted the first performance of Chapí's *La Bruja*. Still later he succeeded Luigi Mancinelli as conductor of the Sociedad de Conciertos in Madrid; he held this post for twelve years. He is a member of the Academia de Bellas Artes and composer of *María del Pilar* and numerous other zarzuelas, including *Las Panderetas*, *El Baile de Luis Alonso*, *La Tempranica*, *El Husar de la Guardia*, and *Cinematógrafo Nacional*.

Other light composers who may be listed are Rafael Calleja, Enrique Brú, Alberto Foglietti, Pablo Luna, Vicente Lleó, and Arturo Saco del Valle.

Of a more serious character is the music of Amadeo Vives, born at Collbato. At the age of 10 he went to Barcelona to study with his brother, a musician in a regimental band. He became an acolyte in a church and his first compositions were written under the influence of the organ music which he then heard. From Barcelona he strayed to Malaga where he became a conductor, and from there he went to Madrid where he played in churches and cafés indifferently, it would seem. At times he was even reduced to peddling on the streets and to writing musical criticism for a Barcelona paper. *Artus* (after a Breton legend), produced in Barcelona in 1897, established his fame. He founded the celebrated Orfeó Catalá in Barcelona, afterwards directed by Millet, and his male choruses written for this organization are said to be among his best works. The list of his operas includes *Don Lucas del Cigarral*, his first attempt at the traditional classic Spanish zarzuela, produced in Madrid in 1899, *Enda d'Uriach*, for which Angel Guimerá wrote the book (Barcelona; 1900); *Colomba* (Madrid; 1910); *Maruxa*, "égloga lírica en 2 actos" (1914); and *Tabaré* (1914), and about thirty zarzuelas including *El Tesoro*, *El Señor Pandolfo*, and *Bohemios*.

Joaquín Larregla was a native of the mountain town of Lumbier in Spanish Navarre. After some schooling at Pamplona he entered the Madrid Conservatory under Zabalza and Arrieta. He has made somewhat of a name both as pianist and composer. He is especially, according to Manuel Manrique de Lara, the composer of Navarre, his works "evoking the landscapes, songs, and traditions of his province." He is a member of the Bellas Artes and an instructor in the Conservatory. His works include *Navarra Montañesa*, *Miguel Andrés*, and *I Viva Navarra!*

The war, it may be suggested, has had a most salutary effect on Spanish music, while it has killed the tonal art in most other countries. It has driven the Spaniards, however, back into their own country and thus may be directly responsible for the foundation of a definite modern school of Spanish music. One of those to leave Paris in 1914 was Manuel de Falla, of whom G.

AMADEO VIVES

Jean-Aubry says, " To-day he is the most striking figure of the Spanish school, to-morrow he will be a composer of European fame, just as is Ravel or Stravinsky."

Manuel de Falla was born at Cadiz, November 23, 1877. He studied harmony with Alejandro Odero and Enrique Broca; later he went to Madrid where he studied piano with José Trigo and composition with Felipe Pedrell. He was still under fourteen when the Madrid Academy of Music awarded him the first prize for his piano playing. Between 1890 and 1904 he divided his time between composing and piano playing, both as soloist and in concerted chamber music. The compositions of this period were not published, however, and now de Falla cannot be urged to speak of them. In 1907 he went to Paris, where, from the very first, he received a warm welcome from Paul Dukas. Debussy was also friendly. His only published works at this were *Quatres Pièces Espagnoles ; Aragonesa, Cubana, Montañesa,* and *Andaluza,* for piano, and *Trois Mélodies ; Les Colombes, Chinoiserie,* and *Seguidille,* words by Théophile Gautier. In 1910 he made his début as a pianist in Paris and the following year in London. . . .

On April 1, 1913, the Casino at Nice produced his first opera, *La Vida Breve* (which so early as 1905 had won a prize at the Madrid Academy of Fine Arts) with Lilian Grenville as Salud ; on December 30, 1913, the work was performed at the Opéra-Comique in Paris with Marguerite Carré as Salud. The first performance of this lyric drama in Spain occurred at the Teatro de la Zarzuela in Madrid, November 14, 1914. *La Vida Breve* has been compared to *Cavalleria Rusticana*, " a *Cavalleria* written by a consummate musician penetrated with a keen desire to express his thoughts without making easy concessions to the mob." ... The orchestration has been warmly praised. " In the first act he has linked the two scenes with an admirable evocation of Granada at dusk ; faint sounds of voices rise from the distant town and all the atmosphere is laden with nonchalance, fragrance, and love."

With the beginning of the war de Falla left France for his native land. He launched *La Vida Breve* in Spain with some success and on April 15, 1915, his second opera, *El Amor Brujo*, was produced at the Lara Theatre in Madrid. Aubry tells us that this work was a failure. However, the composer suppressed the spoken and sung parts, enlarged the orchestration, and made of it a symphonic suite, " semi-Arabian " in style. Pastora Imperio, too, has used this music for her dances.

Aubry pronounces de Falla's *Nocturnes*, produced in Madrid in 1916, the most important orchestral work yet written by a Spaniard. The Spanish title reads : *Noches en los Jardines de España*. There are three parts described by these subtitles : *En el Generalife, Danza Lejana*, and *En los Jardines de la Sierra de Córdoba.* The piano plays an important part in the orchestration but is never heard alone. " The thematic material is built, as in *La Vida Breve* or in *El Amor Brujo* on rhythms, modes, cadences, or forms inspired by but never borrowed from Andalusian folksong."

When the Russian Ballet visited Spain Serge de Diaghileff was so much interested in the work of de Falla that he commissioned him to write a ballet on the subject of Alarcón's novel, " El Sombrero de tres Picos."

Joaquín Turina is another important figure in the modern school. Debussy compared his orchestral work, *La Procesión del Rocio*, to a luminous fresco. In an article in " The Musical Standard," January 6, 1917, Guilhermina Suggia writes : " This work, composed in 1912 and dedicated to Enrique Fernández Arbós, depicts one of those striking processions in honour of the Blessed Virgin Mary of which Richard Ford writes in such picturesque fashion in the old edition of Murray's ' Handbook of Spain ' (1845)." Every year in the month of June, *la procesión del Rocio* takes place, and all the grandees in the town of Seville come out in their carriages to take part in the festivity. Turina has also composed an opera, *Fea y con Gracia* (1905), a string quartet, and numerous works for piano, among which may be mentioned *Trois Danses Andalouses* (*Petenera, Tango,* and *Zapateado*), *Sevilla,* a suite, and

Recuerdos de mi rincón (*Tragedia cómica para piano*).

José María Usandizaga, one of the most promising of the younger composers, died in 1915. He was born in 1888 at San Sebastian and died therefore at the age of 27, one year after his opera, *Las Golondrinas*, was successfully produced at Madrid (February 4, 1914) with the tenor Sagi-Barba in the leading rôle. Usandizaga was a man of exceedingly frail physique, weak and lame, and he died of tuberculosis. He was a pupil, I believe, of Vincent d'Indy. His posthumous opera, *La Llama*, was produced at San Sebastian and Madrid during the winter of 1917-18. Gregorio Martínez Sierra, one of the foremost writers of the younger generation, furnished the books for both his operas.

Enrique (more properly Enrich or Enric; Enrique is the Castilian form of this Catalan name) Morera is, perhaps, the leading Catalan composer. He is best-known for his choral arrangements of folk-songs, some of which have been heard in New York through the medium of the Schola Cantorum, but he has written music for Guimerá's plays, and a lyric drama entitled *L'Alegría que passa*, the book for which was furnished by Santiago Rusiñol.

Conrado del Campo has written a *Divina Comedia* for orchestra and Bartolomé Pérez Casas a *Suite Murcienne* which G. Jean-Aubry includes in a list of modern Spanish orchestral music.

Pérez Casas is at present the conductor of the Philharmonic Orchestra of Madrid. He and Turina conducted the orchestra for the Russian Ballet during the May, 1918, visit of that organization to Madrid.

I have the very pretty *Impressions Musicales* for piano of Oscar Esplá. The subtitle is *Cuentos Infantiles, composición escrita en* 1905 *para una fiesta de niños*. There are five parts which are entitled, respectively, *En el Hogar*, *Barba Azul*, *Caperucita Roja*, *Cenicienta*, and *Antaño*. This music is not very Spanish; indeed it reminds me strongly of the music of Rebikoff.

R. Villar has written many pieces for piano, including *Páginas Románticas*, *Nereida*, *Foot-Ball*, several songs, and pieces for violin and piano and 'cello and piano. V. Costa y Nogueras is the composer of *Flor de Almendro* (1901), *Inés de Castro* (1905), and *Valieri* (1906). J. Gómez is the composer of a *Suite in A* for orchestra which has been arranged for the piano. It includes *Prelude*, *Intermezzo*, *Popular Song*, and *Finale-Dance*.

Enrique Granados was the second* of the important Spanish composers to visit North America. His place in the list of modern Iberian musicians is indubitably a high one; though it must not be taken for granted that *all* the best music of Spain crosses the Pyrenees (for reasons already noted it is evident that some Spanish

---

*Albéniz came to the United States as a pianist in the seventies when he was about fifteen years old,

music can never be heard to advantage outside of Spain), and it is by no means to be taken for granted that Granados was a greater musician than several who dwell in Barcelona and Madrid without making excursions into the outer world. In his own country I am told Granados was admired chiefly as a pianist, and his performances on that instrument in New York stamped him as an original interpretative artist, one capable of extracting the last tonal meaning out of his own compositions for the pianoforte, which are his best work.

Shortly after his arrival in New York he stated to several reporters that America knew nothing about Spanish music, and that Bizet's *Carmen* was not in any sense Spanish. I hold no brief for *Carmen* being Spanish but it is effective, and that *Goyescas* as an opera is not. In the first place, its muddy and blatant orchestration would detract from its power to please (this opinion might conceivably be altered were the opera given under Spanish conditions in Spain). The manuscript score of *Goyescas* now reposes in the Museum of the Hispanic Society, in that delightful quarter of New York where the apartment houses bear the names of Goya and Velazquez, and it is interesting to note that it is a *piano* score. What has become of the orchestral partition and who was responsible for it I do not know. It is certain, however, that the miniature charm of the *Goyescas* becomes more obvious in the piano version, performed by Ernest Schelling or the composer himself, than in the opera house. The growth of the work is interesting. Fragments of it took shape in the composer's brain and on paper seventeen years ago, the result of the study of Goya's paintings in the Prado. These fragments were moulded into a suite in 1909 and again into an opera in 1914 (or before then). F. Periquet, the librettist, was asked to fit words to the score, a task which he accomplished with difficulty. Spanish is not an easy tongue to sing. To Mme. Barrientos this accounts for the comparatively small number of Spanish operas. *Goyescas*, like many a zarzuela, lags when the dance rhythms cease. I find little joy myself in listening to *La Maja y el Ruiseñor* ; in fact, the entire last scene sounds banal to my ears. In the four volumes of Spanish dances which Granados wrote for piano (published by the Sociedad Anónima Casa Dotésio in Barcelona) I console myself for my lack of interest in *Goyescas*. These lovely dances combine in their artistic form all the elements of the folk-dances as I have described them. They bespeak a careful study and an intimate knowledge of the originals. And any pianist, amateur or professional, will take joy in playing them.

Enrique Granados y Campina was born July 27, 1867, at Lerida, Cataluña. (He died March 24, 1916 ; a passenger on the *Sussex*, torpedoed in the English Channel.) From 1884 to 1887 he studied piano under Pujol and composition under Felipe Pedrell at the Madrid Conservatory. That the latter was his master presupposed on his part a valuable knowledge of the treasures of Spain's past and that, I think, we may safely allow him. There is, I am told, an interesting combination of classicism and folk-lore in his work. At any rate, Granados was a faithful disciple of Pedrell. In 1898 his opera *María del Carmen* was produced in Madrid and has since been heard in Valencia, Barcelona, and other Spanish cities. Five years later some fragments of another opera, *Foletto*, were produced at Barcelona. His third opera, *Liliana*, was produced at Barcelona in 1911. He wrote numerous songs to texts by the poet, Apeles Mestres; Galician songs, two symphonic poems, *La Nit del Mort* and *Dante* (performed by the Chicago Symphony Orchestra for the first time in America at the concerts of November 5 and 6, 1915); a piano trio, string quartet, and various books of piano music (*Danzas Españolas*, *Valses Poéticos*, *Bocetos*, etc.).

The Land of Joy

"Dancing is something more than an amusement in Spain. It is part of that solemn ritual which enters into the whole life of the people. It expresses their very spirit."

Havelock Ellis.

The Land of Joy

AN idle observer of theatrical conditions might derive a certain ironic pleasure from remarking the contradiction implied in the professed admiration of the constables of the playhouse for the unconventional and their almost passionate adoration for the conventional. We constantly hear it said that the public cries for novelty, and just as constantly we see the same kind of acting, the same gestures, the same Julian Mitchellisms and George Marionisms and Ned Wayburnisms repeated in and out of season, summer and winter. Indeed, certain conventions (which bore us even now) are so deeply rooted in the soil of our theatre that I see no hope of their being eradicated before the year 1999, at which date other conventions will have supplanted them and will likewise have become tiresome.

In this respect our theatre does not differ materially from the theatres of other countries except in one particular. In Europe the juxtaposition of nations makes an interchange of conventions possible, which brings about slow change or rapid revolution. Paris, for example, has received visits from the Russian Ballet which almost assumed the proportions of Tartar invasions. London, too, has been invaded by the Russians and by the Irish. The Irish playwrights indeed, are continually pounding away at British middle-class complacency. Germany, in turn, has been invaded by England, and we find Max Reinhardt well on his way toward giving a complete cycle of the plays of Shakespeare ; a few years ago we might have observed Deutschland grovelling hysterically before Oscar Wilde's *Salome*, a play which, at least without its musical dress, has not, I believe, even yet been performed publicly in London. In Italy, of course, there are no artistic invasions (nobody cares to pay for them) and even the conventions of the Italian theatre themselves, such as the *Commedia del' Arte*, are quite dead ; so the country remains as dormant, artistically speaking, as a rag rug, until an enthusiast like Marinetti arises to take it between his teeth and shake it back into rags again.

Very often whisperings of art life in the foreign theatre (such as accounts of Stanislavski's accomplishments in Moscow) cross the Atlantic. Very often the husks of the realities (as was the case with the Russian Ballet) are imported. But whispers and husks have about as much influence as the " New York Times " in a mayoralty campaign, and as a result we find the American theatre as little aware of world activities in the drama as a deaf mute living on a pole in the desert of

Sahara would be. Indeed any intrepid foreign investigator who wishes to study the American drama, American acting, and American stage decoration will find them in almost as virgin a condition as they were in the time of Lincoln.

A few rude assaults have been made on this smug eupepsy. I might mention the coming of Paul Orleneff, who left Alla Nazimova with us to be eventually swallowed up in the conventional American theatre. Four or five years ago a company of Negro players at the Lafayette Theatre gave a performance of a musical revue that boomed like the big bell in the Kremlin at Moscow. Nobody could be deaf to the sounds. Florenz Ziegfeld took over as many of the tunes and gestures as he could buy for his *Follies* of that season, but he neglected to import the one essential quality of the entertainment, its style, for the exploitation of which Negro players were indispensable. For the past two months Mimi Aguglia, one of the greatest actresses of the world, has been performing in a succession of classic and modern plays (a répertoire comprising dramas by Shakespeare, d'Annunzio, Sem Benelli, and Giacosa) at the Garibaldi Theatre, on East Fourth Street, before very large and very enthusiastic audiences, but uptown culture and managerial acumen will not awaken to the importance of this gesture until they read about it in some book published in 1950. . . .

All of which is merely by way of prelude to what

I feel must be something in the nature of lyric outburst and verbal explosion. A few nights ago a Spanish company, unheralded, unsung, indeed almost unwelcomed by such reviewers as had to trudge to the out-of-the-way Park Theatre, came to New York, in a musical revue entitled *The Land of Joy*. The score was written by Joaquín Valverde, *fils*,* whose music is not unknown to us, and the company included La Argentina, a Spanish dancer who had given matinées here in a past season without arousing more than mild enthusiasm. The theatrical impressarii, the song publishers, and the Broadway rabble stayed away on the first night. It was all very well, they might have reasoned, to read about the goings on in Spain, but they would never do in America. Spanish dancers had been imported in the past without awakening undue excitement. Did not the great Carmencita herself visit America twenty or more years ago? These impressarii had ignored the existence of a great psychological (or more properly physiological) truth: you cannot mix Burgundy and Beer! One Spanish dancer surrounded by Americans is just as much lost as the great Nijinsky himself was in an English music hall, where he made a complete and dismal failure. And so they would have been very much astonished (had they been present) on the opening night to have witnessed all the scenes of uncontrollable enthusiasm—just as they are described

---

*Valverde died in the City of Mexico, November 7, 1918.

by Havelock Ellis, Richard Ford, and Chabrier—repeated. The audience, indeed, became hysterical, and broke into wild cries of *Ole! Ole!* Hats were thrown on the stage. The audience became as abandoned as the players, became a part of the action.

You will find all this described in " The Soul of Spain," in " Gatherings from Spain," in Chabrier's letters, and it had all been transplanted to New York almost without a whisper of preparation, which is fortunate, for if it had been expected, doubtless we would have found the way to spoil it. Fancy the average New York first-night audience, stiff and unbending, sceptical and sardonic, welcoming this exhibition! Havelock Ellis gives an ingenious explanation for the fact that Spanish dancing has seldom if ever successfully crossed the border of the Iberian peninsula: " The finest Spanish dancing is at once killed or degraded by the presence of an indifferent or unsympathetic public, and that is probably why it cannot be transplanted, but remains local." Fortunately the Spaniards in the first-night audience gave the cue, unlocked the lips and loosened the hands of us cold Americans. For my part, I was soon yelling *Ole!* louder than anybody else.

The dancer, Doloretes, is indeed extraordinary. The gipsy fascination, the abandoned, perverse bewitchery of this female devil of the dance is not to be described by mouth, typewriter, or quilled pen. Heine would have put her at the head of his dancing temptresses in his ballet of *Méphistophéla* (found by Lumley too indecent for representation at Her Majesty's Theatre, for which it was written; in spite of which the scenario was published in the respectable " Revue de Deux Mondes "). In this ballet a series of dancing celebrities is exhibited by the female Méphistophélès for the entertainment of her victim. After Salome had twisted her flanks and exploited the prowess of her abdominal muscles to perfunctory applause, Doloretes would have heated the blood, not only of Faust, but of the ladies and gentlemen in the orchestra stalls, with the clicking of her heels, the clacking of her castanets, now held high over head, now held low behind her back, the flashing of her ivory teeth, the shrill screaming, electric magenta of her smile, the wile of her wriggle, the passion of her performance. And close beside her the sinuous Mazantinita would flaunt a garish tambourine and wave a shrieking fan. All inanimate objects, shawls, mantillas, combs, and cymbals, become inflamed with life, once they are pressed into the service of these señoritas, languorous and forbidding, indifferent and sensuous. Against these rude gipsies the refined grace and Goyaesque elegance of La Argentina stand forth in high relief, La Argentina, in whose hands the castanets become as potent an instrument for our pleasure as the violin does in the fingers of Jascha Heifetz. Bilbao, too, with his

DOLORETES
from a photograph by White

thundering heels and his tauromachian gestures, bewilders our highly magnetized senses. When, in the dance, he pursues, without catching, the elusive Doloretes, it would seem that the limit of dynamic effects in the theatre had been reached.

Here are singers! The limpid and lovely soprano of the comparatively placid Maria Marco, who introduces figurations into the brilliant music she sings at every turn. One indecent (there is no other word for it) chromatic oriental phrase is so strange that none of us can ever recall it or forget it! And the frantically nervous Luisita Puchol, whose eyelids spring open like the cover of a Jack-in-the-box, and whose hands flutter like saucy butterflies, sings suggestive popular ditties just a shade better than any one else I know of.

But *The Land of Joy* does not rely on one or two principals for its effect. The organization as a whole is as full of fire and purpose as the original Russian Ballet ; the costumes themselves, in their blazing, heated colours, constitute the ingredients of an orgy ; the music, now sentimental (the adaptability of Valverde, who has lived in Paris, is little short of amazing ; there is a vocal waltz in the style of Arditi that Mme. Patti might have introduced into the lesson scene of *Il Barbiere ;* there is another song in the style of George M. Cohan—these by way of contrast to the Iberian music), now pulsing with rhythmic life, is the best Spanish music we have yet heard in this country. The whole entertainment, music, colours, costumes, songs, dances, and all, is as nicely arranged in its crescendos and decrescendos its prestos and adagios as a Mozart finale. The close of the first act, in which the ladies sweep the stage with long ruffled trains, suggestive of all the Manet pictures you have ever seen, would seem to be unapproachable, but the most striking costumes and the wildest dancing are reserved for the very last scene of all. There these bewildering señoritas come forth in the splendorous envelope of embroidered Manila shawls, and such shawls! Prehistoric African roses of unbelievable measure decorate a texture of turquoise, from which depends nearly a yard of silken fringe. In others mingle royal purple and buff, orange and white, black and the kaleidoscope! The revue, a sublimated form of zarzuela, is calculated, indeed, to hold you in a dangerous state of nervous excitement during the entire evening, to keep you awake for the rest of the night, and to entice you to the theatre the next night and the next. It is as intoxicating as vodka, as insidious as cocaine, and it is likely to become a habit, like these stimulants. I have found, indeed, that it appeals to all classes of taste, from that of a telephone operator, whose usual artistic debauch is the latest antipyretic novel of Robert W. Chambers, to that of the frequenter of the concert halls.

I cannot resist further cataloguing; details

shake their fists at my memory ; for instance, the intricate rhythms of Valverde's elaborately syncopated music (not at all like ragtime syncopation), the thrilling orchestration (I remember one dance which is accompanied by drum taps and oboe, nothing else !), the utter absence of tangos (which are Argentine), and habaneras (which are Cuban), most of the music being written in two-four and three-four time, and the interesting use of folk-tunes ; the casual and very suggestive indifference of the dancers, while they are not dancing, seemingly models for a dozen Zuloaga paintings, the apparently inexhaustible skill and variety of these dancers in action, winding ornaments around the melodies with their feet and bodies and arms and heads and castanets as coloratura sopranos do with their voices. Sometimes castanets are not used ; cymbals supplant them, or tambourines, or even fingers. Once, by some esoteric witchcraft, the dancers seemed to tap upon their arms. The effect was so stupendous and terrifying that I could not project myself into that aloof state of mind necessary for a calm dissection of its technique.

What we have been thinking of all these years in accepting the imitation and ignoring the actuality I don't know ; it has all been down in black and white. What Richard Ford saw and wrote down in 1846 I am seeing and writing down in 1917. How these devilish Spaniards have been able to keep it up all this time I can't imagine. Here we have our paradox. Spain has changed so little that Ford's book is still the best to be procured on the subject (you may spend many a delightful half-hour with the charming irony of its pages for company). Spanish dancing is apparently what it was a hundred years ago; no wind from the north has disturbed it. Stranger still, it depends for its effect on the acquirement of a brilliant technique. Merely to play the castanets requires a severe tutelage. And yet it is all as spontaneous, as fresh, as unstudied, as vehement in its appeal, even to Spaniards, as it was in the beginning. Let us hope that Spain will have no artistic reawakening.

Aristotle and Havelock Ellis and Louis Sherwin have taught us that the theatre should be an outlet for suppressed desires. So, indeed, the ideal theatre should. As a matter of fact, in most playhouses (I will generously refrain from naming the one I visited yesterday) I am continually suppressing a desire to strangle somebody or other, but after a visit to the Spaniards I walk out into Columbus Circle completely purged of pity and fear, love, hate, and all the rest. It is an experience.

From George Borrow to Mary Garden

> *" Les femmes disent qu'elle est laide,*
> *Mais tous les hommes en sont fous :*
> *Et l'archevêque de Tolède*
> *Chante la messe à ses genoux."*
>
> Théophile Gautier's " Carmen."

From George Borrow to Mary Garden

(*Histoire sommaire de Carmen*)

ALICE, it will be recalled, adventured into Wonderland bearing a morsel of mushroom in each hand; now she munched one piece, which made her grow tall, now the other, which diminished her height. In this manner she adjusted her size to that of the various doorways and gates of the place as well as to that of the creatures she encountered. In somewhat the same fashion George Borrow, sent by the British Bible Society to distribute the Holy Word in the papalized peninsula, advanced into Spain. In one hand he held a Castilian version of the New Testament; in the other his very considerable curiosity. Doubtless he made many valiant attempts to hawk Bibles, but it is quite as certain that he never restrained his natural aptitude for the companionship of thieves, gitanos, contrabandists, and bandits. More than once his zeal in behalf of the Scriptures landed him in jail, but I can scarcely accept this as proof of his devotion to a holy cause when I remember that he had been attempting in vain to persuade certain Madrid officials to permit him to voluntarily incarcerate himself so that he might have such further opportunities for the pursuit of his studies of the " crabbed gitano " as intercourse with the prisoners might offer. As a matter of fact when he was arrested the English Ambassador secured his pardon before the day was done, but this Borrow refused to consider. He was in jail and he proposed to remain there, and remain he did, a matter of several weeks, during which period he had lengthy talks with all the prisoners, adding substantially to his foreign vocabularies. . . . His sympathy, indeed, was with the gitanos ; he ate and drank and slept with them, sometimes in stables, sometimes in dirty lofts. If he himself did not connive at the " affairs of Egypt," at least he travelled with those who did ; if he did not assist at robberies or murders, he was often aware that they were about to be committed. On one occasion he held converse, which is delightfully recorded, with Sevilla, the picador, whom Prosper Mérimée met and who is referred to in Richard Ford's " Gatherings from Spain." . . . We must, on the whole, thank the British Bible Society for giving Borrow the opportunity to write two strangely charming books, one of them a masterpiece, but over what Borrow did for the Bible Society it is perhaps just as well to draw a shade.

The production of two such books as " The

Zincali " and " The Bible in Spain " may be regarded, however, as sufficient justification for the incorporation and continued existence of the British Bible Society. If all the information he gives us concerning the gipsies in these books is not authentic we may at least be certain that Borrow had a better opportunity for making it so than that afforded any other writer. If, therefore, he has sometimes distorted facts it is because he is first of all an artist and " The Bible in Spain " is first of all a work of art. These books appeared in the early forties and were read and admired all over Europe, awakening an interest in the Iberian Peninsula, and more especially in the Spanish gipsies, which has never since died. In the preface to the second edition of " The Zincali " Borrow relates his astonishment at the success of his book : " the voice not only of England but of the greater part of Europe, informing me that I had achieved a feat—a work in the nineteenth century with some pretensions to originality." And when a writer in " The Spectator " called " The Bible in Spain " " a 'Gil Blas' in water-colours " Borrow fairly bubbled.

" The Zincali " was translated into several languages, among others into French, and among those influenced and affected by it was Prosper Mérimée ; indeed it now seems probable that without the spur of this suggestive book Mérimée would never have written " Carmen," assuredly not in its present form. Here are the facts: Mérimée visited Spain in 1830 and it was during this tour that the Condessa de Teba related to him a story of jealousy and murder, substantially that of "Carmen," in which, however, the gipsies played no part. This material offered scant inspiration for the production of a masterpiece. Mérimée, indeed, seems to have dropped the idea out of his mind entirely until Borrow's books appeared, reviving his interest in the gipsies and suggesting to him the possibility of transferring the Condessa's tale into a gipsy setting. Borrow's translation of the Gospel of Luke into Caló was issued in 1837. There is evidence that Mérimée read it. "The Zincali" came out in London in 1841; "The Bible in Spain" in 1842. "Carmen" first appeared, without the final chapter on the gipsies, in the "Revue des Deux Mondes" for October 1, 1845. The proofs of Mérimée's indebtedness to Borrow are manifold; one of the best is his own admission in his correspondence with his *Inconnue ;* " You asked me the other day where I had obtained my acquaintance with the dialect of the gipsies. I had so many things to tell you that I forgot to reply. I got it from Mr. Borrow; his book is one of the most curious I have read." But the internal evidence is even stronger: all but two of the gipsy proverbs in "Carmen" are to be found in "The Zincali" as is many a detail in plot and description. Professor George T. Northup of the University of

Toronto has traced a number of such resemblances and you may find his account of them in " Modern Philology " for July, 1915. " When he (Mérimée) set out to manufacture local colour he seldom dispensed with literary aid. He did indeed frequently dispense with direct observation," writes Professor Northup. " In his study of the Gipsies Borrow was Mérimée's important, although not his sole, literary guide; and of that a careful comparison of the two works leaves not the slightest doubt."

On one point, however, Mérimée is at variance with Borrow, and this is a most important point, so important, indeed, that the French author, in spite of (perhaps because of !) his obligation to the Englishman, points the finger of scorn at him in the added chapter (largely made up of facts to be found in " The Zincali " !) of " Carmen." Here is the passage : " M. Borrow, missionaire anglais, auteur de deux ouvrages fort intéressants sur les bohémiens d'Espagne, qu'il avait entrepris de convertir, aux frais de la Societé biblique, assure qu'il est sans exemple qu'une Gitana ait jamais eu quelque faiblesse pour un homme étranger à sa race." Borrow does not say *sans exemple ;* " The Gitanas have in general a decided aversion to the white men ; some few instances, however, to the contrary are said to have occurred." Let us continue with Mérimée : " Il me semble qu'il y a beaucoup d'exagération dans les éloges qu'il accorde à leur chasteté. D'abord, le plus grand nombre est dans le cas de la laide d'Ovide : *Casta quam nemo rogavit*. Quant aux jolies, elles sont comme toutes les Espagnoles, difficiles dans le choix de leurs amants. Il faut leur plaire, il faut les mériter."

This is what Borrow has to say about the matter in " The Zincali " : " There is a word in the Gipsy language to which those who speak it attach ideas of peculiar reverence, far superior to that connected with the name of the Supreme Being, the creator of themselves and the universe. This word is *Lácha*, which with them is the corporeal chastity of the females ; we say corporeal chastity, for no other do they hold in the slightest esteem ; it is lawful amongst them, nay praiseworthy, to be obscene in look, gesture, and discourse, to be accessories to vice, and to stand by and laugh at the worst abominations of the Busné (Busno is the term used by the Spanish gipsies for the Spaniard or indeed any person not a gipsy), provided their *Lácha ye trupos*, or corporeal chastity remains unblemished. The Gipsy child, from her earliest years, is told by her strange mother that a good Calli need only dread one thing in this world, and that is the loss of *Lácha*, in comparison with which that of life is of little consequence, as in such an event she will be provided for, but what provision is there for a gipsy who has lost her *Lácha ?* ' Bear this in mind, my child,' she will say, ' and now eat this bread, and go forth and see what you can steal.'"

" A Gipsy girl is generally betrothed at the age of fourteen to the youth whom her parents deem a suitable match, and who is generally a few years older than herself. Marriage is invariably preceded by betrothment. . . . With the Busné or Gentiles, the betrothed female is allowed the freest intercourse, going whither she will, and returning at all times and seasons. With respect to the Busné, indeed, the parents are invariably less cautious than with their own race, as they conceive it next to an impossibility that their child should lose her *Lácha* by any intercourse with *the white blood* ; and true it is that experience has proved that their confidence in this respect is not altogether idle. The Gitanas have in general a decided aversion to the white men ; some few instances, however, to the contrary are said to have occurred."

The gitanas, Borrow goes on to explain, are never above exciting passion in the Busné which, however, they refuse to satisfy. Their dances for the most part are lascivious and obscene. They often act as procuresses. But let no Busno presume from these facts that he may count on a more intimate acquaintanceship. Richard Ford in " Gatherings from Spain " in his description of the *romalis* supports Borrow in his theory : " However indecent these dances may be, yet the performers are inviolably chaste, and as far at least as ungipsy guests are concerned, may be compared to iced punch at a rout ; young girls go through them before the applauding eyes of their parents and brothers, who resent to the death any attempt on their sisters' virtue."

Mérimée refers to the matter in a letter to the *Inconnue;* "What he (Borrow) relates of the gipsies is perfectly true, and his personal observations are entirely in accord with mine save on a single point. In his capacity of clergyman (*sic*), he may very well have deceived himself where I, in my capacity of Frenchman and layman, was able to make conclusive experiments." In spite of the weight of Mérimée's personal experience it may be noted that the majority of Spanish writers are in accord with Borrow, who was *not* a clergyman. And, as Professor Northup slyly points out, the man who taught Isopel Berners of Mumpers Dingle to conjugate the verb "to love" in Armenian may not have been so naïve an observer after all.

Whether gipsies are corporeally chaste or not* is, however, a matter of the slightest moment in relation to the masterpiece that Mérimée based on the theory that they are not. As Havelock Ellis so precisely puts it: "Art is in its sphere

---

*It must be remembered that Mérimée and Borrow were writing nearly a century ago; what was true then may not be true to-day. Borrow, himself, says (in "The Zincali"): "It is, of course, by intermarriage alone that the two races will ever commingle, and before that event is brought about, much modification must take place amongst the Gitanas, in their manners, in their habits, in their affections, and their dislikes, and, perhaps, even in their physical peculiarities; much must be forgotten on both sides, and everything is forgotten in the course of time."

as supreme over fact as Science in its sphere is supreme over fiction. The artist may play either fast or loose with Science, and the finest artist will sometimes play loose." It may be remarked that in general Borrow was more inclined to play loose than Mérimée.

It is interesting enough to realize that " The Bible in Spain," in itself a masterpiece, was the inspiration for another masterpiece, one of the great short stories of all literature. Curiously enough still a third masterpiece emerged from the activities of the British Bible Society, *Carmen*, the opera. In transferring the story to the stage Messrs. Meilhac and Halévy, in searching for dramatic emphasis, have thrown overboard a good deal of the wild and wanton atmosphere, the calid passion, the brutal austerity of the original tale. Carmen, in their version, becomes a mixture of Spanish gipsy and Parisian cocotte. In certain scenes, such as that of the Seguidilla and the duet in the last act a good deal of Mérimée's feeling has been preserved but the scene of the quintet in which the other gipsies taunt Carmen with being *amoureuse* is probably essentially Parisian. So, too, perhaps, is the scene of the Habanera. Spaniards have long protested against the work because, as nearly as I can discover, they consider it an *idealization*. Spanish women as a rule make the worst Carmens, although they have often achieved notable successes in another Spanish character, Rosina in

The Barber of Seville.* An understanding of the French opéra-comique form is essential to a fine interpretation of this gipsy heroine ; even a good deal of the music is not essentially Spanish. If it were it would probably not be great because Bizet was a Frenchman and must perforce in writing French opera hear Spain with French ears. . . . Nevertheless I see no reason why a singer should not go to Mérimée for many hints ; indeed I think she might even go farther and study Borrow's conception of the Spanish gipsy character. One line alone in Mérimée would suggest a new interpretation to an actress capable of realizing it. José is speaking : " Monsieur, quand cette fille-là riait, il n'y avait pas moyen de parler raison. Tout le monde riait avec elle." But an actress must conceive any part in terms of her own personality and this effect could be made only by a very complete *charmeuse*.

In the original story the bull-fighter, Lucas, scarcely appears and he is a picador not an *espada* as he becomes in the opera under the new name of Escamillo. Why was this name changed ? I have a theory, unsupported by any evidence, that Bizet asked his librettists to furnish him with a name which would fit the music of the marvellous duet in the last act. He probably had achieved the phrase which now accompanies *Ah ! je t'aime, Escamillo*, only to discover that it could not be

---

*Nevertheless *Carmen* is frequently sung in Spain, even in Seville, although probably more often in Italian than in French or Spanish.

married to the name Lucas. Jealousy remains the motive for the murder of Carmen although the scenes are quite differently arranged in the tale and in the lyric drama. . . . Micaela is new. The only suggestion of her in Mérimée's story is the following line of José's : " J'étais jeune alors ; je pensais toujours au pays, et je croyais pas qu'il y eut de jolies filles sans jupes bleues et sans nattes tombant sur les épaules." Carmen's second meeting with José does not take place at Lillas Pastia's but the third does, and ever so many details such as the " chaine avec du fil de laiton," the cassia which the hussy removes from her lips to toss at José's feet, the rejected ring, etc., are incidents from Mérimée. Why, one wonders, does not some interpreter remember that the original Carmen broke a plate and from the pieces fashioned castanets to play while she danced the *romalis* for José ? . . . The brutal Garcia le Borgne, Carmen's *rom*, disappears completely. He is not essential to the intrigue devised by the librettists. They have also blotted out Carmen's very diverting adventures with the Englishman at Gibraltar.

Carmen was produced at the Paris Opéra-Comique March 3, 1875. The first performance was coldly received. Charles Pigot (Bizet's biographer) informs us that the prelude to the second act was repeated; the air of the Toreador and the quintet were applauded : that was all. The curtain fell on each act to complete indifference. The discouragement of the composer seems to have been deep. We do not wonder at it. Vincent d'Indy told Edmond Galabert that after the first act he and a group of young musicians met Bizet on the sidewalk near the stage entrance of the theatre and felicitated him on the life and colour in the music. Bizet responded: "Vous êtes les premiers qui me disiez ça, et je crains bien que vous ne soyez les derniers." *Carmen* was a failure. The reviews were bad. There were, curiously enough, many charges of immorality. Pigot assures us that Camille du Locle, the director of the theatre, who never believed in *Carmen*, was more or less responsible for these. To a minister who wrote in asking for a loge for the first night he replied that it would perhaps be better if he came to the general rehearsal to see if he found the piece sufficiently respectable for his wife and daughters! . . . Possibly these charges of immorality awakened curiosity. At any rate it is certain that after the fifth performance the receipts rose and the apathy of the audiences became less marked. The piece was given for the thirty-seventh time on June 13, just before the theatre closed for the summer. Bizet had died June 3. In the fall *Carmen* was revived and given thirteen representations; then not again in Paris until 1883.

At various times attempts have been made to prove that *Carmen* did not fail when it was first produced. The most notable of these is an article contributed to the "Ménestrel" (1903; p. 53) by Arthur Pougin entitled "La Légende de la Chute de *Carmen* et la Mort de Bizet" in which he quotes Mme. Galli-Marié : " L'insuccès de *Carmen* à la création, mais c'est une légende ! *Carmen* n'est pas tombée au bout de quelques représentations, comme beaucoup le croient. . . . Nous l'avons jouée plus de quarante fois dans la saison, et quand ce pauvre Bizet est mort, le succes de son chef d'œuvre semblait definitivement assis." . . . Pigot scoffs at this, pointing out that the exigencies of the répertoire often make it necessary for a director to perform a work oftener than it will pay to do so. His evidence is cumulative and for the most part convincing.

According to H. Sutherland Edwards, who seems to have acquired this information from Marie Roze, in its original form the opera included two complete airs for Carmen which, in the end, the composer and his librettists decided to suppress. The gipsy was to have been represented as capable of remorse (!) and after the scene in which she foretells her death by the cards was to be left alone to give vent to her feelings in a pathetic air ! The other omitted air occurred in the last act.

Mr. Edwards gives us more details : The bullfight, according to the original design of the authors, was to be shown in the form of a tableau, occupying all the back of the stage with live chorus figures and " supers " in the front of the picture and painted figures behind them. Escamillo was to have been seen triumphing over the figure of the fallen bull, while the crowd of spectators overlooking the arena shouted vociferously the air of the Toreador. In a dark background (the back of the stage alone being illuminated) the figures of Carmen and Don José were to be seen.

Charles Pigot tells us that Micaela's song was composed originally for *Griselidis* (an opera for which Sardou supplied the book and which Bizet never completed). The score of *Carmen* would be perfect without it. The story of the Habanera is related elsewhere in this volume (p. 27), and need not be repeated here.

Carmen originally contained a good deal of spoken dialogue, which is still to be heard at the Paris Opéra-Comique. Guiraud (not Godard, as Clara Louise Kellogg has it) wrote the music for the recitatives and it is with these that the work is usually performed in foreign theatres, including the Metropolitan Opera House. In some theatres, however, a bastard version, a combination of these two forms, is given.

It is probable that Spaniards base their main objection to *Carmen* on the idealization of a national type offered by the libretto. It is not likely that they object to the music. At any rate they have always found Italian, French, and German music pleasant to their ears and many Spanish composers have been less Spanish than Bizet, who, after all, was a Jew, and something of an oriental himself! The dances and some of the entr'acte music, then, of this opera may be considered thoroughly Spanish. But Spanish or not there is no denying that Bizet succeeded in writing one of the most delightful of operas. When I first read Nietzsche's " The Case of Wagner " I was inclined to feel that the German in his rage against Wagner had put up the silliest of opponents against him in order to make his ex-hero more ridiculous. I do not feel that way to-day. I humbly subscribe to all of Nietzsche's outpourings : " This music seems to me to be perfect. It approaches lightly, nimbly, and with courtesy. It is amiable, it does not produce *sweat*. ' What is good is easy ; everything divine runs with light feet '—the first proposition of my Aesthetics. This music is wicked, subtle, and fatalistic ; it remains popular at the same time,—it has the subtlety of a race, not of an individual. It is rich. It is precise. . . . It has borrowed from Mérimée the logic in passion, the shortest route, *stern* necessity. It possesses, above all, what belongs to the warm climate, the dryness of the air, its *limpidezza*. . . . This music is gay ; but it has not a French or a German gaiety. Its gaiety is African ; destiny hangs over it, its happiness is short, sudden, and without forgiveness." Has any one ever described *Carmen* so well ? And there is much more. I pray you, turn to " The Case of Wagner " and read it all . . . and perhaps begin to believe, as I do, that aside from *Tristan* Wagner himself never penned so complete a masterpiece.

Before we begin to glance at some of the ladies who have attempted to do justice to the Spanish gipsy it might be well to pause for a few seconds on two descriptions of the *cigarrera* type. Gautier visited the celebrated Fábrica de Tobacos in Seville, where Carmen was employed until she began to stick knives into her co-workers. Here is what he says of it :

"L'on nous conduisit aux ateliers où se roulent les cigares en feuilles. Cinq ou six cents femmes sont employées à cette préparation. Quand nous nîmes le pied dans leur salle, nous fumes assailis par un ouragan de bruits : elles parlaient, chantaient et se disputaient toutes à la fois. Je n'ai jamais entendu un vacarme pareil. Elles étaient jeunes pour la plupart, et il y en avait de fort jolies. Le néligé extrême de leur toilette permettait d'apprécier leurs charmes en toute liberté. Quelques-unes portaient résolument à l'angle de leur bouche un bout de cigare avec l'aplomb d'un officier de hussards ; d'autres, ô muse, viens à mon aide ! d'autres . . . chiquaient comme de vieux matelots, car on leur laisse prendre autant de tabac qu'elles en peuvent consommer sur place. . . . La *cigarrera* de Séville est un type, comme la *manola* de Madrid."

I also append Edmondo de Amicis's description : "The women are almost all in three immense rooms, divided into three parts, by three rows of pilasters. The first effect is stupendous. Eight hundred girls present themselves at once to your view. They are divided into groups of five or six, and are seated around work-tables, crowded together, those in the distance indistinct, and the last scarcely visible. They are all young, but few are children ; in all, eight hundred dark heads of hair, and eight hundred dusky faces from every province of Andalusia, from Jaen to Cadiz, and from Granada to Seville. You hear the buzzing that you would in a square full of people. The walls, from one end of the three rooms to the other, are covered with skirts, shawls, handkerchiefs, and scarfs, and, curiously enough, the whole mass of rags, which would be sufficient to fill a hundred second-hand shops, presents two predominating colours, both continuous, one above the other, like the stripes of a flag. The black of the shawls is above, the red of the dresses below, and mixed with the latter, are white, purple, and yellow, so that you seem to see an immense fancy costume shop, or a large dancing-room, in which the ballet girls, in order to obtain more freedom of movement, have hung everything on the wall which is not absolutely necessary to cover them decently. The girls put on these dresses when they leave, but wear old things while at work, which, however, are white and red like the others. The heat being insupportable, they lighten their clothing as much as possible, so that among those five thousand there may be hardly fifty whose arms or shoulders the visitor will not have the opportunity of admiring at his leisure, without counting the exceptional cases which present themselves quite unexpectedly in passing from one room to the other, behind the doors, columns, or in distant corners. There are some very beautiful faces, and even those that are not absolutely beautiful, have something about them which attracts the eye and remains impressed upon the memory—the colouring, eyes, brows, and smile, for instance. Many, and especially the so-called *gitane*, are dark brown, like mulattoes, and have protruding lips; others have such large eyes that a faithful likeness of them would seem an exaggeration. The majority are small, well made, and all wear a rose, pink, or a bunch of field flowers among their braids."*

Mlle. Célestine Galli-Marié was the first Carmen. She is said to have been delightful, but the first interpreter of a part always has an advantage over those who follow her; she need not fear comparison. She was charged with immorality, but it is not likely that she allowed herself as many gipsy liberties as some of her successors. Charles Pigot tells us that she took advantage of Mérimée's vigorous etching: " elle avait pris modèle sur ce portrait d'une ressemblance qui donne le

*There is a picturesque account of this Fábrica de Tabacos in Baron Ch. Davillier's " Espagne " (Hachette; Paris; 1874).

frisson de la vie au personnage évoqué. Oeillades assassines, regards chargés de volupté qui livrent la victime pieds et poings liés, déhanchements lascifs, poings sur la hanche, rien ne manquait à la ressemblance ; et ce déploiement de perversités physiques, refletant à merveille l'âme de cette bohémienne ehontée, cette crudité de tons dans le rendu du geste et de l'allure qui choquèrent bien des personnes et firent crier a l'immoralité, étaient indiqués par l'effronterie du personnage, et, j'ajouterai, nécessaires à la verité du drame, à l'explication de l'ensorcellement subit du navarrais."

Arthur Pougin says of her : " Mme. Galli-Marié should take rank with those numerous artists who, although endowed with no great voice, have for a century past rendered to this theatre services made remarkable by their talent for acting and their incontestable worth from a dramatic point of view. . . . Equally capable of exciting laughter or of provoking tears, endowed with an artistic temperament of great originality . . . which has permitted her making out of parts confided to her distinct types . . . in which she has represented personages whose nature and characteristics are essentially opposed." . . . She died at Vence, near Nice, September 22, 1905.

Fräulein Ehnn seems to have been the second Carmen ; as Vienna was the second city to produce Bizet's opera ; the date was October 23, 1875. Brussels had the honour of being the third city ;

the date was February 8, 1876; Mlle. Maria Dérivis enacted the rôle of the gipsy here. Thereafter the opera made the grand tour of the world, and firmly established itself in the répertoire even of the meanest singing theatres. Scarcely a singer but has at one time or other sung one of the rôles in this work. Sometimes it has been Micaela (Mme. Melba, among others, has sung this rôle); sometimes Frasquita, in which Emma Trentini made an instantaneous impression in New York, more often than not Carmen herself, for contraltos and sopranos have both appeared in the part.

Adèle Isaac, a soprano, sang the part when *Carmen* was revived at the Opéra-Comique in 1883. She did not make a very good impression but the opera was received much more favourably than it had been in 1875. When Mme. Galli-Marié reappeared she was again deemed matchless. Then came Mme. Nardi. About 1888 Mme. Deschamps-Jehin sang the rôle. Mme. Tarquini d'Or succeeded her. In December, 1892, Mme. Calvé disclosed her characterization. It has been the custom in America to signalize a vast distinction between her early and late performances of the rôle; it has been said that she became self-conscious and wayward. Paris always found her so, but it must be remembered that tradition must be followed in the French theatre. Charles Darcourt's criticism in "Le Figaro" the morning after her début in the part, is enough to give a

Parisian impression : He reproached her " d'être allée trop loin dans ses gestes et ses attitudes, d'avoir été trop peu comme il faut, d'être sorti des limites du bon gout et surtout du bon ton."
. . . Mlle. Charlotte Wyns sang Carmen in 1894. Mme. Nina Pack, Mme. de Nuovina and Mme. Marie Brema followed her. In 1898 came Georgette Leblanc, who subsequently became the wife of Maurice Maeterlinck, and who still later divorced him, Mlle. Leblanc's interpretation was a new one and she inspired one critic (Fierens-Gevaert) to put on paper the following ecstatic lines about her appearance in the second act :

" Mlle. Leblanc is clothed in a long robe of plaited tulle, ornamented with spangles. Her body, finely proportioned, is revealed by this indiscreet drapery. Her nobly modelled shoulders and arms are bare. Her hair is confined by three circles of gold, arranged in Grecian fashion. Alma, gipsy, daughter of the East, princess of the harem, Byzantine empress or Moorish dancer ? All this is suggested by this fantastic and seductive costume. But a more ideal image pursues us. The singer is constantly urged by feminine visions of our ultra-modern poets. She finds absolute beauty in the exquisite body of a woman animated by a Florentine robe. And it is through this imaginary figure that she composes her other incarnations ; and in a tavern where gipsy women meet soldiers, she evokes the apparition of a woman of Mantegna or Botticelli, degraded, vile, who gives the idea of a shameless creature that has not lost entirely the gracefulness of her original rank. She is never weary of cheapening her original model. She is sensual, impudent, voluptuous, gross, but in her white diction, in her blithe walk, you divine her desire of evoking something else. . . . Carmen is, according to Mlle. Leblanc, a hybrid, monstrous creature. You look upon her with eager curiosity and infinite sadness. . . . Mlle. Leblanc makes light of her voice. She maltreats it, threshes it, subjects it to inhuman inflections. . . . Her singing is not musical, her interpretation lacks the naïveté necessary to true dramatic power. Nevertheless, she is one of the most emotional interpreters of our period. Her limited abilities, hidden by a thousand details in accentuation, remind one of the weak and ornate poetry of artistic degeneration. . . . Thanks to her, Antioch and Alexandria, corrupt and adorable cities, live again, for an hour."

Perhaps Philip Hale's description of Carmen owes something to this picture of Mlle. Leblanc. At any rate it is striking enough to reproduce:

" Carmen lived years before she was known to Mérimée. She dies many deaths and many are her resurrections. When the world was young, they say her name was Lilith, and the serpent for her sake hated Adam. She perished that wild night when the heavens rained fire upon the cities

ZULOAGA'S PORTRAIT OF LUCIENNE BRÉVAL AS CARMEN, ACT II
By permission of the Hispanic Society of America

of the plain. Samson knew her when she dwelt in the valley of Sorek. The mound builders saw her and fell at her feet. She disquieted the blameless men of Ethiopia. Years after she was the friend of Theodora. In the fifteenth century she was noticed in Sabbatic revels led by the four-horned goat. She was in Paris at the end of the last century and she wore powder and patches at the dinner given by the Marquis de Sade. In Spain she smoked cigarettes and wrecked the life of Don José."

Georgette Leblanc's successors were Mme. Delna, Zélie de Lussan, Marié de l'Isle (who sang Mercedes before she sang Carmen), Cécile Thévenet, Jenny Passama, Claire Friché, Marguerite Sylva, Mme. Lafargue, Mlle. Vix, Mlle. Brohly, Mlle. Charbonnel, Sigrid Arnoldson, Mlle. Mérentié, and Lucienne Bréval, whom Zuloaga painted twice in the part. One of these paintings hangs in the Metropolitan Museum of Art in New York. The other belongs to Mme. Bréval. I have not seen Mme. Bréval in *Carmen* but I have seen her in other operas and I think I am safe in saying that Zuloaga's conception of her is more gipsy-like than her performance. . . . One of the latest of the Paris Carmens has been Mary Garden.

I think Col. Mapleson brought *Carmen* to London. The first performance was given June 22, 1878, at Her Majesty's Theatre. He was fortunate in having as his leading interpreter Minnie Hauk of Brooklyn, who, I believe, had been heard in the part in Brussels before she sang it in London. She is said to have been fascinating in the rôle and straightway made it pretty much her own. Mapleson in his " Memoirs " tells what a time he had with the other interpreters. Campanini returned the part of José, giving as his explanation that he had no romance and no love duet except with the *seconda donna*. Del Puente suggested that the part of Escamillo must have been intended for one of the chorus. Mlle. Valleria made a similar remark in regard to Micaela. However, the wily Colonel managed to get the singers to come to a rehearsal or two and in a short time they became infatuated with their rôles.

It has been generally taken for granted and indeed you will find it so stated in most of the books, that Minnie Hauk was the first American Carmen, but Clara Louise Kellogg in her " Memoirs " denies this, asserting that she preceded Miss Hauk here in the rôle by several months.* One thing is certain, that Miss Hauk made more of an impression as Carmen on her contemporaries than Mme. Kellogg. An early international exponent of the rôle was Marie Roze, who according to H. Sutherland Edwards, at first could scarcely be persuaded

---

*According to W. J. Henderson (in his introduction to *Carmen*; Dodd, Mead and Co., 1911), who is usually as accurate as anybody can be about such matters, " *Carmen* was first performed in New York (in Italian) at the Academy of Music, October 23, 1878, under the management of Col. J. H. Mapleson. The principal singers were Minnie Hauk as Carmen, Italo Campanini as Don José, and Giuseppe del Puente as Escamillo." However it should be noted that Mme. Kellogg does not say that she was the first *New York* Carmen.

to undertake a character of so vile a nature. She finally succumbed to the lure, however. Edwards says of her : " Marie Roze brought forward the gentle side of the character. Carmen has something of the playfulness of the cat, something also of the ferocity of the tigress ; and the ferocious side of Carmen's disposition could not find a sympathetic exponent in Madame Marie Roze." Clara Louise Kellogg gives us, as is her wont, a more forceful description : " When she (Marie Roze) was singing *Carmen* she was the gentlest mannered gipsy that was ever stabbed by a jealous lover—a handsome Carmen but too sweet and good for anything."

Christine Nilsson is said to have decided that the rôle was not pure enough for her, but Adelina Patti, who has stated publicly that Wagner wrote *Parsifal* for her and that she refused the rôle of Kundry, could not forego the chance to appear as the Mérimée-Bizet gipsy. Her failure was abysmal. H. E. Krehbiel says she was seen " and occasionally heard " in the part. She " ignored its dramatic elements entirely, and cared only for the music, and only for the music in which she sang alone." But Pauline Lucca sang the part with success, I believe.

Carmen was a rôle that Lilli Lehmann had frequently sung in Germany before she came to America and she made her American début in the part. Here is Mr. Krehbiel's description of her performance (" Chapters of Opera ") :

"Lehmann as the gipsy cigarette maker, with her Habanera and Seguidilla, with her errant fancy wandering from a sentimental brigadier to a dashing bull-fighter, is a conception which will not come easy to the admirers of the later Brünnhilde and Isolde; and, indeed, she was a puzzling phenomenon to the experienced observers of that time. Carmen was already a familiar apparition to New Yorkers, who had imagined that Minnie Hauk had spoken the last word in the interpretation of that character. When Fräulein Lehmann came her tall stature and erect, almost military, bearing, were calculated to produce an effect of surprise of such a nature that it had to be overcome before it was possible to enter into the feeling with which she informed the part. To the eye, moreover, she was a somewhat more matronly Carmen than the fancy, stimulated by earlier performances of the opera or the reading of Mérimée's novel, was prepared to accept; but it was in harmony with the new picture that she stripped the character of the flippancy and playfulness popularly associated with it, and intensified its sinister side. In this, Fräulein Lehmann deviated from Mme. Hauk's impersonation and approached that of Mme. Trebelli. . . . In her musical performance she surpassed both of those admired and experienced artists."

Zelia Trebelli, referred to in the last paragraph, was a popular Carmen here in the eighties, but it was not until Emma Calvé appeared at the

Metropolitan Opera House in 1893-4 that *Carmen* became a fetish. The Frenchwoman so completely fascinated the public in this rôle that she was seldom allowed to appear in any other, although her Santuzza, her Cherubino, her Anita, and her Ophélie were probably more artistic achievements. She was beautiful and wanton and wayward and thoroughly fascinating when she first appeared here in the rôle. Whether she became enamoured of herself in it later, or merely tired of it, does not appear to be certain ; at any rate she allowed her mannerisms full sway and soon completely stepped out of the picture, the more completely as she frequently distorted the rhythms of the music. Calvé had the power, as few singers have possessed it, to colour her voice to express different emotions, and her vocal treatment of the part in the beginning was a delight. Her costumes were very wonderful. I have read criticisms of her and other Carmens, bearing on this point. But Carmen was a smuggler, a thief, even a murderess ; she often had plenty of money, and she frequently dressed extravagantly. Mérimée does not leave us any room for doubt in this matter. The second time José sees her she is described thus : " Elle était parée, cette fois, comme une châsse, pomponnée, attifée, tout or et tout rubans. Une robe à paillettes, des souliers bleus à paillettes aussi, des fleurs et des galons partout."

How many Carmens have we seen since Calvé !

Zélie de Lussan, who gave an exquisite opéra-comique performance, with a touch of savagery and a charming sense of humour! Fanchon Thompson, who attempted to sing the part in English with Henry W. Savage's company at the Metropolitan Opera House but who broke down and left the stage after she had sung a few bars. Olive Fremstad, who had appeared in the part many times in Munich (all contraltos sing the part in Germany; even Ernestine Schumann-Heink has sung it there) was the Metropolitan Opera House Carmen for a season or two. Her interpretation followed that of Lilli Lehmann. It was very austere, almost savage, and with very little humour. Olive Fremstad was applauded in the rôle but she never succeeded in making the opera popular.

But Clotilde Bressler-Gianoli sang the part fifteen times in Oscar Hammerstein's first Manhattan Opera House season; the performance of *Carmen* at this theatre, indeed, saved the first season, as Mary Garden and Luisa Tetrazzini saved the second. Mme. Bressler-Gianoli, who had been heard at the Paris Opéra-Comique in the rôle, and indeed once with the New Orleans Opera Company at the New York Casino, gave a delightful interpretation; its chief charm was its absolute freedom from self-consciousness; it was so natural that it became real. Calvé sang the part four times at the end of this season. Mme. Gerville-Réache was another Manhattan Opera House Carmen and Lina Cavalieri was a fourth.

OLIVE FREMSTAD AS CARMEN, ACT I
from an early photograph by Lützel, Munich

Mme. Cavalieri was particularly charming in the dances, but she made a very unconvincing gipsy. In no part that she has ever played before or since has she produced such an impression of girlish innocence. Mariette Mazarin sang Carmen here before she was heard in *Elektra*. Her Carmen was brazen and diabolic, electric and strident ; I think it might be included among the great Carmens ; it was very original. Marguerite Sylva's Carmen is traditional and pleasant ; in tone very like that of Zélie de Lussan. It has been sufficiently appreciated. . . . Maria Gay, the Spanish Carmen, attempted realistic touches such as expectoration ; a well-sung, well-thought-out, consistent performance, but lacking in glamour.

Although the Century Theatre with Kathleen Howard and others, and sundry small Italian companies had offered Carmen in New York the work was missing from the répertoire of the Metropolitan Opera House for several seasons until Geraldine Farrar brought it back in 1914-15.* The

*Mr. Henderson gives an interesting and probably authentic reason for the disappearance of *Carmen* from the répertoire of the Metropolitan Opera House : " It has not been performed as much in America in recent seasons as it has in Europe because American audiences have learned to expect a very striking impersonation of the heroine and do not eagerly go to hear the opera when such an impersonation is not offered." And again : " Mme. Calvé's bold, picturesque and capricious impersonation of the gipsy became the idol of the American imagination, and thereby much harm was wrought, for whereas the gifted performer began the season with a consistent and well-executed characterization, she speedily permitted success to turn her head and lead her to abandon genuine dramatic art for catch-penny devices directed at the unthinking. The result has been that opera-goers have found correct impersonations of Carmen uninteresting."

scenery and costumes were new. By way of caprice the Spanish soldiers were dressed in Bavarian blue although José is referred to as *canari* in the text. Caruso sang José, as he had with Mme. Fremstad, and Mr. Toscanini conducted. With the public Carmen has become one of Mme. Farrar's favourite rôles, sharing that distinction with Butterfly.

Other Carmens who may be mentioned are Anna de Belocca, Stella Bonheur, Kirkby-Lunn, Ottilie Metzger, Emmy Destinn, Marie Tempest, Selina Dolaro, Camille Seygard, Alice Gentle, Eleanora de Cisneros, Jane Noria, Ester Ferrabini, Margarita d'Alvarez, Tarquinia Tarquini. . . . It might be said in passing that some Carmens do not get nearer to the Giralda Tower in Seville than Stanford White's imitation in Madison Square.

Although Mary Garden brought to America three of the best parts in her répertoire, Mélisande, Thais, and Louise, eight rôles, at least, she has sung for the first time in this country, Natoma, Dulcinée in *Don Quichotte*, Prince Charmant in *Cendrillon*, Salome, Jean in *Le Jongleur de Notre Dame*, Gismonda, Cléopâtre, and Carmen. She first identified herself with the Spanish gipsy at the Philadelphia Opera House on November 3, 1911. On February 13, 1912, with the Philadelphia Company, she was heard in Bizet's opera in New York. I attended both of these performances and found much to admire in each of them. Something, however, was lacking; something was wrong; nobody seemed to know exactly what. The general impression was that Mary Garden had failed at last and it was generally bruited about that she would never sing Carmen again. However, Miss Garden is not one of those who permits herself to fail; it may be that she remembers Schumann's saying, "He who sets limits to himself will always be expected to remain within them." . . . In any case I was not surprised to learn that Miss Garden was singing Carmen at the Opéra-Comique in Paris during the season of 1916-17. In the fall of 1917 she sang the part in Chicago and on February 8, 1918, with the Chicago Opera Company, she reappeared in the part in New York. This occasion may be regarded as one of the greatest triumphs a singer has ever achieved. For Mary Garden had so entirely reconceived the rôle, so stepped into its atmosphere, that she had now made it not merely one of her great parts (it ranks with her Mélisande, her Monna Vanna, and her Thais) but also she had made it *her* part. There is indeed no Carmen of the moment who can be compared with her.

A feral gipsy from Triana, this apparition; a *cigarrera* in the Fàbrica de Tabacos for the sake of the " affairs of Egypt "; a true gitana in her *saya* " with many rows of flounces." Any day in the streets of Seville could you have seen her like, peering through the gratings into the patios, ready to tell *bahi*. " Eyes of a gipsy, eyes of a wolf " is a Spanish proverb, according to Mérimée, and Borrow tells us that a gitano can always be detected by his eye : " Its peculiarity consists chiefly in a strange staring expression, which to be understood must be seen, and in a thin glaze which steals over it when in repose, and seems to emit phospheric light." . . . So, did it seem to me, had become the eyes of Mary Garden. This discinct creature, instinctively paradoxical, would be equally at home in the spinnies of the arid Spanish plains, on the dirty stage of a *maison de danses* at Triana, or, gaily bedecked and spangled, like a " bedizened butterfly of commerce " in a box of the Plaza de Toros. Sensuous and caline, as in the Seguidilla, rubbing her velvet back against the *canari* ; proud and magnetic (she must have carried a piece of the *bar láchi* about with her), she drew her lovers to her side ; she did not advance to meet them. White hot in anger : other Carmens have hurled the helmet after the departing José ; Mary Garden *shot* it at him like a bursting hand grenade. Fatalist : cabalistic signs smouldering in purple flame on her breast, in the end published this motto in Roman letters : " *Je ne crains rien !* " When she danced she scarcely lifted her feet from the floor, tapping her heels rhythmically and sensuously into the hidden chambers of our brains ; so the inquisitors maddened their victims with the endless drop, drop, drop of water. Her manipulation of her fan, a monstrous Spanish fan, coral on one side and with tauromachian decorations on the other, was in itself a lesson in diabolic grace. She made the fan a part of herself, a part of her movement, as a Spanish woman would. . . . The climax was fitting enough; her answer to José in the last act, "*Non, je ne t'aime plus*," sung not with force, not in anger, but with a sort of amused contempt. . . So does the gipsy regard the busno . . . *with a sort of amused contempt*. Fatalist, humourist, enchantress, panther, savage, *gamine*, in turn, this Carmen suggested the virgin brutality of Spain, the austere portentous passion of Persephone, the frivolous devilments of Hell itself.

Index

Abencérages, Les, 28
Africanistas, Los, 92
Aguglia, Mimi, 117
Aidá, 35
Alarcón, Pedro de, 27, 107
Albéniz, Isaac, 10, 13, 14, 40, 53, 83, 92, 93, 97, 98, 100, 101, 109
d'Albert, Eugen, 28
Alegría de la Huerta, 76
Alegría que Passa, l', 108
Alhambra, En la, 95
Alhambra, The, 41
d'Alvarez, Margarita, 10, 156
Amante Astuto, l', 8
Amantes de Teruel, Los, 94
America para los Americanos, 9 n
Amicis, Edmondo de, 58, 72 n, 142
Amor Brujo, El, 36, 106
Amores de un Principe, 95
Amour en Espagne, l', 100
Angeles, Los, 94
d'Annunzio, Gabriele, 117
Apocalipsis, El, 95
Apolo Theatre, Madrid, 75, 76, 102
Aqui Hase Farta un Hombre, 93

Aragonaise, 26
Arbell, Lucy, 26
Arbore de Diana, l', 85
Arbós, Enrique Fernández, 14, 83, 99, 107
Arditi, Luigi, 121
Argentina, La, 11, 35, 60, 100, 118, 120
Arnoldson, Sigrid, 149
Arriaga, J. C., 86
Arrieta, Emilio, 9 n., 77, 88, 96, 100, 104
Artus, 103
Azara, 28

Bach, 14
Baile de Luis Alonso, 103
Baillot, 86
Balakirew, 18, 99
Balfe, Michael William, 27
Bandurria, 45
Bara, Theda, 11
Barberillo en Orán, El, 95
Barbiere di Siviglia, Il, 28, 121, 136
Barbieri, F. A., 88, 89
Barrientos, Maria, 11, 111
Bauer, Harold, 22
Beethoven, 14, 15, 27, 30, 83, 92

INDEX

Beidler, Franz, 99
Bellaigue, Camille, 13, 90
Bellini, 83 n
Belocca, Anna de, 156
Benavente, Jacinto, 35, 102
Benavente (comp.), 79
Benelli, S., 117
Berlioz, 37
Bermudo, Father, 30
Bilbao, 120
Bizet, Georges, 11, 25, 53, 110, 138, 139, 140, 156
Blasones y Talegas, 94
Boabdil, 9
Bocetos, 112
Bohemios, 104
Bolero, 44, 62
Bonheur, Stella, 156
Bori, Lucrezia, 9, 12
Boris Godunow, 15, 91, 92
Borrow, George, 127 *sqq.*
Bos, Coenraad V., 19
Botticelli, 148
Brassin, Louis, 97
Brema, Marie, 147
Bressler-Gianoli, C. 154
Bretón, Tomás, 45 *n.*, 53, 94, 95
Bréval, Lucienne, 149
Broca, Enrique, 105
Brohly, Mlle., 149
Brú, Enrique, 103
Bruckner, 92
Bruja, La, 93, 94, 103
Bruneau, Alfred, 43
Bull-fight, 72, 136, 139
Busoni, 18, 92

Caballero, F., 75, 77, 79, 92
Cabezón, 32
Cabo Primero, El, 77, 92
Cachucha, 44
Calderas de Pedro Botero, Las, 93
Calderon, 74
Calleja, Rafael, 103
Calvé, Emma, 19, 146, 153, 154, 155 *n.*
Camargo, Marie-Anne, 44
Campanadas, Las, 93
Campanero de Begoña, 95
Campo, Conrado del, 13, 108
Cancan, 84
Canción del Olvido, La, 102
Canción del Soldado, La, 102
Capriccio Espagnole, 17
Capricciosa Corretta, La, 85
Carmen, 12, 20, 24, 25, 110, 127 *sqq.*, 140, 154, 155
"Carmen," 129 *sqq.*
Carmencita, 9, 118
Caro-Delvaille, H., 70
Carré, Marguerite, 106
Caruso, Enrico, 156
Casals, Pablo, 11, 19
Casas, Pérez, 13, 108, 109
Caseda, 32
Castanets, 34, 35, 48, 123
Castillo, 32
Catalonia, 13, 97
Cavalieri, Lina, 154, 155
Cavalleria Rusticana, 106
Celestina, La, 13, 90
Centro de la Tierra, El, 100
Certamen de Cremona, 95

INDEX 163

Certamen Nacional, 77
Cervantes, 26, 28
Chabrier, E., 16, 17, 36, 38, 45, 46, 49, 67, 78, 83, 119
Chambers, R. W., 122
Chapí, Ruperto, 9 n., 53, 77, 92, 94, 102, 103
Chaplin, Charles, 12
Charbonnel, Mlle., 149
Chérubin, 25
Cherubini, 28, 86
Chieftain, The, 28
Chopin, 98, 99
Chorley, H. F., 27 n.
Chueca, Federico, 77, 100
Cid, Le, 25, 26, 28
Cinematógrafo, Nacional, 103
Circe, 93
Cisneros, Eleanora de, 94, 156
Cisterna Encantada, 88
Clavel Rojo, El, 95
Clément and Larousse, 25
Cleopatra, 90
Cohan, George M., 121
Collet, H. E., 31
Colomba, 104
Combat, The, 99
Conchita, 19
Conquista de Granada, 88
Conquistador, Le, 22
Copeland, George, 10, 97
Corelli, 43
Corona contra Corona, 95
Corregidor, Der, 27
Cosa Rara, La, 85
Costa y Nogueras, V., 109

Covadonga, 95
Cura del Regimiento, El, 93
Curzon, Henri de, 90
Cygne, Le, 44
Czarina, La, 93

Dalcroze, Jaques, 66, 92
Dama del Rey, La, 88
Dama Roja, La, 93
Danse Macabre, 95
Dante, 99, 112
Darcourt, Charles, 146
Dargomisky, 28
Davillier, Baron, C., 61 n., 144 n.
Debussy, Claude, 17, 19, 20, 99, 105, 107
"Declaración de Instrumentos," 30
Delibes, Léo, 19
Delna, Marie, 149
Del Puente, Giuseppe, 150
Demófilo, 69
De Madrid á Biarritz, 88
Dérivis, Maria, 146
Deschamps-Jehin, Mme, 146
Desrat, 61
Destinn, Emmy, 156
Deux Contrats, 87
Deyo, Ruth, 19
Diaghilew, Serge de, 107
Diaz, Rafael, 11 n.
Dineros del Sacristan, 92
Divina Comedia, 13, 108
Doctor of Alcantara, 28
Dolaro, Selina, 156

INDEX

Dolores, La, 7, 14, 94
Doloretes, 54, 119, -21
Domingo de Ramos, El, 95
Doña Juana la Loca, 96
Don Carlos, 28
Don César de Bazan, 25
Don Gil, 95
Don Giovanni, 28, 86
Donizetti, 28
Don Juan, 19
Donna Diana, 28
Don Lucas del Cigarral, 104
Don Quichotte, 25, 26
Don Quixote, 19, 25, 26, 92
Doré, Gustave, 61 *n.*
Drei Pintos, Die, 28 *n.*
Dukas, Paul, 105
Dupont, Joseph, 97
Durón, Sebastian, 32, 79

Echegaray, José, 74, 96
Echegaray, Miguel, 74, 92, 95
Edad en la Boca, La, 88
Edwards, H. S., 139, 150, 151
Edwards, Rhoda G., 57
Ehnn, Fräulein, 145
Eichberg, Julius, 28
Elektra, 155
Elgar, Sir Edward, 92
Ellis, Havelock, 15, 34, 39, 41, 44, 46, 65, 72 *n.*, 78, 119, 124, 134
Elssler, Fanny, 10, 44, 51
Encina, Juan del, 80, 81
Enda d'Uriach, 104
Enemigos Domesticos, 88
Enrico Clifford, 98

Entre Rocas, 93
Epitalame, 99
Erlanger, Camille, 28
Ermitage Fleurie, l' 98
Ernani, 27
Escenas Andaluzas, 95
Escenas de Capa y Espada, 94
Esclavos Felices, Los, 86
Eslava, 30, 31, 87, 92, 95, 96
Esplá, Oscar, 109
España, 16, 17
Estampes, 19
Estudiantina, 19

Falla, Manuel de, 13, 36, 100, 104, 105 *sqq.*
Falstaff, 91
Fandango, 45, 60, 61, 62, 63
Farrar, Geraldine, 11, 12, 155, 156
Farrega, 40
Fassett, Jacob S., Jr., 27 *n.*
Fauré, Gabriel, 24
Faviani, Mme., 44
Favorita, La, 28
Fazzoletto, 87
Fea y con Gracia, 107
" Femme et le Pantin," 20
Feria, The, 42
Fernández, Lucas, 81
Ferrabini, Ester, 156
Ferrer, Miguel, 79
Fétis, 81, 86, 87
Fidelio, 9, 27
Fierens-Gevaert, 147
Figlia dell'Aria, La, 8
Filles de Cadix, Les, 19

INDEX

Filmore, John C., 38
Finck, H. T., 49, 58, 72 *n*.
Flor de Almendro, 109
Florestan, 87
Foglietti, Alberto, 103
Foletto, 112
Folias, 43
Ford, Anne, 64
Ford, Richard, 35, 39, 41, 53, 72 *n*., 83, 107, 119, 123, 128, 133
Forza del Destino, 28
Franck, 99
Fremstad, Olive, 19, 154, 156
Friché, Claire, 149
Friedenthal, Albert, 39
Fuertes, M. S., 30, 42, 45, 72, 79, 80, 92

Gainsborough, T., 63, 64
Galabert, Edmond, 138
Galeotes, Los, 95
Gallarda, 42, 43
Galli-Marié, Célestine, 25, 139, 144, 145, 146
Garcia, Manuel, 8, 24, 25, 86, 87, 92
Garcia, Manuel, fils, 92
Garcia, Maria, *v*. Malibran
Garden, Mary, 26, 149, 154, 156, *sqq*.
Garibaldi Theatre, N.Y., 117
Garin, 95
Garrison, Mabel, 71
Gatti-Casazza, Giulio, 8, 12
Gautier, Théophile, 50, 52, 72 *n*., 83 *n*., 105, 125, 142

Gay, Maria, 12, 155
Gaztambide, Joaquin, 88
Geibel, F., 19
Gendarmes, Los, 93
Gentle, Alice, 156
Gerville-Réache, Mme., 154
Giacosa, 117
Gibert, 99
Gigantes y Cabezudos, 75, 77, 92
Giménez, Gerónimo, 102
Giroflé-Girofla, 28
Glinka, 18
Gloria y Peluca, 89
Godard, 140
Gogorza, Emilio de, 9
Golondrinas, Las, 13, 108
Gomes, 32
Gomez, Antonio Carlos, 8
Gómez, J., 109
Gonzalo de Córdoba, 96
Gounod, Charles, 24
Goya, 11, 12, 110, 111
Goya, La, 36
Goyescas, 7, 9 *n*., 11, 74, 110, 111
Granados, Enrique, 10, 11, 13, 31, 53, 74, 86 *sqq*., 99, 109
Gran Via, La, 8, 75, 78, 100
Greco, El, 12
Grenville, Lilian, 105
Grieg, Edvard, 98
Griselidis, 140
Grove, Sir G., 15, 16, 45, 65, 74
Guarany, Il, 8

INDEX

Guerrero, Francisco, 32
Guimerá, Angel, 104, 108
Guiraud, 140
Guitares et Mandolines, 19
Guzmán el Bueno, 95

Habanera, 25, 39, 42, 48, 123, 135, 140, 152
Habanera, La, 17, 20, 21, 23
Hale, Edward Everett, 72 *n.*
Hale, Philip, 24, 44, 45, 61, 148
Hamilton, H. V., 74, 79, 82
Hammerstein, Oscar, 7, 9, 10, 154
Hampa, 44
Handel, 65
Harrigan, 77
Harris, Frank, 72 *n.*
Hauk, Minnie, 149, 150, 152
Hay, John, 72 *n.*, 83 *n.*
Heifetz, Jascha, 120
Heine, 120
Henderson, W. J., 150 *n.*, 155 *n.*
Hesperia, 93
Heugel, 25
Heure Espagnole, l', 27
Hidalgo, 79
Hidalgo, Elvira de, 10
Hija de Jefté, La, 93
Hijas de Zebedeo, Las, 92
Howard, Kathleen, 155
Hugo, Victor, 90
Humperdinck, E., 18
Huneker, James, 97
Husar de la Guardia, 103

Iberia (Albéniz), 97, 98, 99
Iberia (Debussy), 17, 20
Ildegonda, 88
Images, 17
Imperio, Pastora, 35, 36
Impressions Musicales, 109
d'Indy, V., 108, 138
Inés de Castro, 109
Irene de Otranto, 96
Iriarte, Tomás de, 61 *n*
Irving, Washington, 19
Isaac, Adèle, 146
Isle, Marié de l', 149
I Viva Navarra, 104

Jacara, 43, 81
Jadassohn, 97
Jardin de Falerina, El, 79
Jean-Aubrey, J., 13, 98, 105, 106, 108
Joachim, 99
Jot, Alben, 45
Jota, 18, 26, 45, 46, 67, 78
Jota, La, 20, 21
Juan Francisco, 93
Juanes, Juan de, 32
Juarez, 32
Jugar con Fuego, 89
Juicio de Friné, El, 96

Kellogg, Clara, 140, 150, 151
Kirkby-Lunn, Mme, 156
Krehbiel, 37, 38, 42, 151
Kufferath, F., 97
Kutznezoff, Mme., 12

INDEX

Lacome, P., 45, 69
Lafargue, Mme., 149
Lafontaine, Rev. H. Cart de, 56, 74, 83
Lalo, Edouard, 18
Lana, 79
Land of Joy, The, 9 *n.*, 14, 76, 77, 102, 118
Laparra, Raoul, 7, 20, 21, 22, 24, 53
Lara, Manrique de, 93, 104
Larregla, Joaquín, 104
Lavignac, Albert, 15
Lazaro, Hipolito, 11 *n.*
Leblanc, Georgette, 147, 148, 149
Lecocq, 28, 73
Lehmann, Lilli, 151, 152, 154
Lewes, G. H., 82 *n.*
Leyenda del Monje, La, 93
Liliana, 112
Liszt, 18, 44, 97, 99
Llama, La, 102, 108
Lleó, Vicente, 103
Llobet, Miguel, 11, 40
Lobo, 32
Locle, Camille du, 138
Loeffler, Charles Martin, 19
Lombard, Louis, 15
Lopez-Chavarri, E., 14, 89
Los Seises, 58
Louys, Pierre, 20
Lucca, Pauline, 151
Lumley, Benjamin, 120
Luna, Pablo, 103
Lussan, Zélie de, 149, 154, 155

Mackinlay, Sterling, 24
Madrileños, Los, 93
Maeterlinck, M., 147
Magic Opal, The, 97
Mahler, Gustav, 92
Maison de Danses, La, 100
Maitland, J. A. Fuller, 91
Maja de Numbo, La, 96
Maja y el Ruiseñor, La, 111
Malagueña, 47, 48, 52, 60
Mal de Amores, El, 102
Malibran, Mme., 8, 87
Mancinelli, Luigi, 103
Mandoline, 19
Manet, Edouard, 122
Mantegna, 148
Manuel Venegas, 27
Mapleson, J. H., 149, 150
Marchant, William, 15
Marco, Maria, 121
Mardones, José, 11 *n.*
Margarita la Tornera, 93
Maria del Carmen, 112
Maria del Pilar, 103
Marín, F. Rodriguez, 69
Marina, 9 *n.*, 77, 89
Marinetti, F. T., 116
Marion, George, 115
Maritana, 28
Marmontel, 97
Martin y Solar, 85, 86
Maruxa, 104
Massenet, 24, 25
Matilda y Malek Adel, 88
Matinada, La, 90
Maurische Rhapsodie, 18
Mazantinita, 120

INDEX

Mazarin, Mariette, 155
Mazeppa, 90
Meilhac & Halévy, 135 sqq.
Mejorana, La, 35
Melba, Nellie, 146
Meller, Raquel, 36
Mendès, Catulle, 43
Méphistophéla, 120
Mérentié, Mlle., 149
Mérimée, Prosper, 128 sqq.
Merlin l'Enchanteur, 98
Mestres, Apeles, 112
Metzger, Ottilie, 156
Miguel Andrés, 104
Milagro de la Virgen, El, 93, 103
Millet, Lluis, 70, 71, 103
Mitchell, Julian, 115
Mithradates, 96
Molière, 54
Molina, Amalia, 35, 36
Molinos de Viento, Los, 96
Montez, Lola, 10
Moorish Fantasy, 94
Morales, Christofero, 31, 32
Morera, Enrique, 70, 108
Mort du Tasse, La, 87
Moszkowski, 9, 18
Moullé, Edouard, 46
Mozart, 28, 86, 122
Muck, Dr. Karl, 95
Mulligan Guards' Ball, 77
Murillo, 32
Musorgsky, 15, 92, 98

Nadal, Juan, 11 n.
Nardi, Mme., 146
Navarraise, La, 25, 26
Navarra Montañesca, 104
Navarro, 32
Navas, Juan de, 79
Naves de Cortés, Las, 93
Nazimova, Alla, 117
Negro Actors, 117
Ni Amor se Libra de Amor, 79
Nieto, Manuel, 77
Nietzsche, 141
Night in Madrid, A, 18
Nijinsky, Waslav, 118
Nilsson, Christine, 151
Nin, J. Joachim, 101
Nit del Mort, La, 112
Noblet, Mlle., 44, 51
Noches en los Jardines de España, 13, 106
Noria, Jane, 156
Northup, G. T., 130, 131, 134
Nozze de Figaro, Le, 28
Nuovina, Mme. de, 147

Ocôn, Cecilio, 69
Odero, Alejandro, 105
Offenbach, 73, 84 n.
Ole, 44, 53
d'Or, Tarquini, Mme., 146
Orfeó Catalá, 70, 71, 103
Orleneff, Paul, 117
Ornstein, Leo, 10, 97, 101
Otero, 10
Overture on a Theme of a Spanish March, 18

Pack, Nina, 147
Paesiello, 26

INDEX

Pahissa, 99
Paine, John Knowles, 28
Palestrina, 31, 32, 92
Palomares, 79
Panderitas, Las, 103
Pareda y Barreto, José, 30
Parsifal, 7, 28, 91, 151
Paseo, 23
Passama, Jenny, 149
Patti, Adelina, 121, 151
Pavana, 42, 43
Pavlowa, Anna, 10, 44
Paz, Señora, 11
Pedrell, Felipe, 13, 14, 31, 32, 33, 69, 70, 79, 80, 84, 89, 90, 91, 105, 112
Pedro el Cruel, 87
Pélleas et Mélisande, 7
Peña y Goñi, Antonio, 80
Penfield, Edward, 72 *n*.
Pepita Jiménez, 98
Periquet, F., 111
Petenara, 22, 47, 70
Petrella, 102
Peyró, José, 79
Piccinni, 26
Pickpockets' Jota, 8 *n*.
Pigot, Charles, 25, 137, 138, 140, 144
Pireneos, Los, 14, 89, 90
Pobre Valbuena, El, 9 *n*.
Poème Espagnole, 19
Poeta Calculista, El, 87
Poiret, Paul, 11
Polaire, 100
Polo, 44
Ponte, da, 85

Pougin, A., 87, 139, 145
Pozo, 70
Preciosa, 28
Primera Salida de Don Quijote, La, 96
Procesión del Rocio, 13, 107
Puchol, Luisita, 121
Puig y Alsubide, J., 69
Pujol, Juan B., 99
Puñao de Rosas, 9 *n*., 77
Purcell, Henry, 26
Pushkin, 28

Quasimodo, 90
Quintero Brothers, 35, 102
Quittard, Henry, 70

Ragtime, 123
Ramirez, Anita, 36
Rapsodie Espagnole, 19
Raquel, 95
Ravel, Maurice, 19, 26, 27, 53, 101, 105
Reclamo, El, 93
Reina Mora, La, 102
Reinhardt, Max, 116
Rey que Rabio, El, 93
Reznicek, 28
Rhythmes Espagnoles, 22
Ribera, 32
Riemann, Hugo, 26
Rimsky-Korsakow, 17, 28
Risco, Juan, 79
Robles, Garcia, 99
Rockstro, 16, 31
Roda, Cecilio de, 26
Rodriguez, Isabel, 12

170 INDEX

Roger de Flor, 93
Rojes, Victor, 35
Romalis, 53
Romero, 32
Rose of Castile, The, 27
Rose de Grenade, La, 73, 100
Rossini, 28
Roze, Marie, 139, 150, 151
Rubinstein, A., 18, 19, 97
Rueda, 23, 46
Rueda de la Fortuna, 92
Rusiñol, Santiago, 108
Russian Ballet, 107, 115, 116

Saint-Saëns, Camille, 19, 44, 94, 95
Saldoni, Baltasar, 88, 89
Salieri, 26
Sallilas, 44
Salome, 26
Saltus, Edgar, 72 n.
San Antonio de la Florida, 98
Sanborn, Pitts, 20, 40
"Sapateados", 47
Sarabanda, 42
Sarasate, Pablo de, 18, 88
Sardou, 140
Sargent, 9
Sati, Erik, 101
Scheherazade, 18
Schelling, Ernest, 10, 97, 111
Schindler, Kurt, 71
Schumann, Robert, 18, 99
Schumann-Heink, E., 154
Secreto de la Reina El, 88
Seguidilla, 45, 69, 152, 158
Segurola, Andres de, 9, 12

Selva Sin Amor, La, 79
Señas del Archiduque, 88
Señor Pandolfo, El, 104
Séré, Octave, 27
Serrano, Emilio, 96
Serrano, José, 102
Sevilla, 128
Sevillana, 23, 45, 48, 56, 57
Seygard, Camille, 156
Shakespeare, 117
Sherwin, Louis, 124
Sierra, G. M., 108
Slaviansky, Dmitri, 70
Smetana, 92
Soirée dans Grenade, La, 19
Solea, 23
Soledas, 47
Solitario, El, 87
Sorcière, La, 28
Sorolla, 9
Soubies, A., 29, 30, 32, 79, 81
Southgate, Dr. T. L., 15
Spanisches Liederbuch, 18
Spanisches Liederspiel, 18
Spanish Dances, 18
Spanish Rhapsody, 18
Stanislavski, 116
Stein, Gertrude, 43
Stanley, Helen, 24
Statue Guest, The, 28
Strauss, Richard, 19, 92
Stravinsky, Igor, 116
Suggia, Guilhermina, 107
Suite Murcienne, 13, 108
Sullivan, Sir Arthur, 28
Supervia, 12
Svendsen, 19

INDEX 171

Sylva, Marguerite, 149, 155
Symons, Arthur, 28 n., 54, 58
Symphonie Espagnole, 18

Tabaré (Bretôn), 95
Tabaré (Vives), 104
Tabernera de Londres, 89
Taglioni, 10
Tango, 12, 34, 47, 48, 78, 123
Tango de la Menegilda, 8 n.
Tango et la Malagueña, 22
Tannhaeuser, 15
Tarquini, Tarquinia, 20, 156
Tarrega, 40
Tasso d Ferrara, El, 90
Teba, Condessa de, 130
Tebaldini, G., 32
Tempest, Marie, 156
Tempestad, La, 9 n., 93
Tempranica, La, 103
Tesoro, El, 104
Tesrai, Dolores, 44
Tetrazzini, Luisa, 92, 154
Thévenet, Cécile, 149
Thicknesse, P., 62 sqq.
Thomas, Ambroise, 102
Thompson, Fanchon, 154
Tiefland, 28
Tientos, 23
Tirana, 44
Tonadilla, 82
Toreador and Andalusian, 18
Torpadie, Greta, 19
Torre, Jerónimo de la, 79
Torres, J. Romero de, 35
Tortajada, La, 10
Toscanini, Arturo, 156

Towers, John, 26, 92
Trebelli, Zelia, 152, 153
Tregua del Ptolemaide, 87
Trigo, José, 105
Tristan und Isolde, 91
Trovatore, Il, 27
Turina, Joaquin, 10, 13, 107, 109

Ultimo Abencerraje, El, 90
Underhill, J. G., 73 n., 75, 76, 101
Usandizaga, José Maria, 13, 102, 108

Valera, 34
Valieri, 109
Valle, Arturo Saco del, 103
Valle de Andorra, El, 88
Valleria, Mlle., 150
Valverde, Joaquín, 12, 75
Valverde, Joaquin, fils, 73, 100, 101, 118, 121, 123
Vega, Lope de, 74, 79
Velasquez, 32, 110
Verbena de la Paloma, 77, 94
Verdi, 27, 28
Viaje d Cochinchina, 89
Via Libre, 93
Victoria, T. L. de, 31, 32, 100
Vida Breve, 13, 105, 106
Vieuxtemps, 99
Villancicos, 81
Villar, R., 109
Viñes, Ricardo, 101
Vives, Amadeo, 70, 103
Vix, Genevieve, 149

INDEX

Vuelta del Corsario, La, 89
Vuiller, Gaston, 61 *n*.
Vuillermoz, Emile, 21, 70

Wagner, Richard, 28, 50, 72 *n*., 91, 141, 142, 151
Waldteufel, 17, 19
Wallace, W. V., 28
Wayburn, Ned, 115
Weber, 28
Whistler, 88
White, Stanford, 156
Wilde, Oscar, 116
Wolf, Hugo, 18, 27
Wood, Sir Henry J., 97
Wyns, Charlotte, 147

Xacara, 43

Yradier, Sebastian, 25

Zabalza, 96, 104
Zandonai, 19
Zarabanda, 42
Zarzuela, 9 *n*., 14, 72, 73, 74, 75, 76, 77, 78, 79, 80, 82, 84, 88, 89, 92, 94, 96, 100, 101, 102, 103, 104, 111, 122
Ziegfeld, Florenz, 117
Zorahayda, 19
Zuloaga, 9, 36, 123, 149
Zurbaran, 32

For Product Safety Concerns and Information please contact our EU
representative GPSR@taylorandfrancis.com
Taylor & Francis Verlag GmbH, Kaufingerstraße 24, 80331 München, Germany

www.ingramcontent.com/pod-product-compliance
Lightning Source LLC
Chambersburg PA
CBHW061446300426
44114CB00014B/1854